John Hunter is a Consultant Physician at Addenbrooke's Hospital, Cambridge and a recognized authority on the subject of food allergy and intolerance. He developed an interest in food in relation to diseases of the gut in response to the need of the many sufferers of irritable bowel syndrome attending his out-patients' clinic. He has contributed over 40 research papers to major medical journals including the *Lancet, Update* and the *British Medical Journal*.

Virginia Alun Jones has been research fellow to Dr Hunter at Addenbrooke's since 1982. As well as contributing to this book, she has presented the results of the team's work at scientific meetings in this country and Europe. She too has written numerous articles for among others the *British Medical Journal*, the *Lancet*, and the *Journal of the Royal College of General Practitioners*.

Elizabeth Workman gained her State Registration as a dietitian after following the dietetics course at Leeds Polytechnic, already being a holder of a biological sciences degree from Leicester University. She has gained great expertise in helping people with food-related diseases over the last 4 years and enjoys the challenge of devising appetizing and nutritious recipes from unusual ingredients, not least because her husband is a vegetarian and she caters for a growing family.

POSITIVE HEALTH GUIDE

THE
ALLERGY
DIET

How to overcome your food intolerance

Elizabeth Workman, SRD
John Hunter, MD
Virginia Alun Jones, MD

Foreword by James L. Achord, MD
Professor and Director
Division of Digestive Diseases
University of Mississippi

LAROUSSE

Published in the U.S. in 1985 by Larousse & Co, Inc.
572 Fifth Avenue, New York, New York.

First published in the United Kingdom in 1984
by Martin Dunitz Ltd, London

ISBN 0 88332 454 7 (h/b)
ISBN 0 88332 455 5 (p/b)

Phototypeset in Garamond by Bookens, Saffron Walden, Essex

Printed by Toppan Printing Company (S) Pty Ltd, Singapore

Front cover *photograph shows: Strawberry ice (top right, see page 106), Feta salad (top left, see page 55), Apple-walnut teabread and Crusty rolls (bottom left, see pages 92 and 91), Roast chicken (bottom right, see page 74)*
Back cover *photograph shows: The devil's own drumsticks (top, see page 65), Apple and bean salad (bottom, see page 52)*

CONTENTS

FOREWORD

James L. Achord, MD,
Professor and Director, Division of Digestive Diseases, University of Mississippi

Dr Hunter and his colleagues have tackled a difficult problem in this book. Because each of us has had extensive experience with eating we feel qualified as experts on the subject, and physicians are no exception. Even the dullest of us is aware that in some people, eating certain foods causes unpleasant symptoms but symptoms, even rather severe ones, do not necessarily indicate disease or even permanent impairment. In fact, many symptoms produced by food intolerance can also be caused by emotional factors. This is why the authors in the very first pages have carefully distinguished between food allergy, actually an uncommon disease, and food intolerance. While some diseases are accompanied by food intolerance, most symptoms produced by certain foods reflect no specific known disease. This knowledge, however, does not make symptoms any the less hurtful. This book is about food intolerance, how to discover and manage it, not about disease.

Since most of us like to feel that we are in control of our own mental and physical well-being, it is deceptively easy to conclude that by manipulating our diet we can control all manner of things happening within us. This can lead to all sorts of bizarre eating behavior which the authors generally caution us against by some very sound advice. This includes checking with your physician to be sure that your symptoms are not due to something that requires a different treatment and, perhaps even more important, being sure that the diet you settle upon, if any, is adequate in nutrition and essential vitamins and minerals. To this I would add that in the US there are now legions of 'food experts' who give themselves various scientific-sounding titles and are anxious to provide you with all sorts of generally unnecessary food supplements and advice (for a price, of course), not all of which is as healthy for you as it is for their purse.

I come to that part of this book which makes up the larger bulk. The list of menus and instructions on preparations of special foods is hard to come by and will be of inestimable aid to those who have a need for them. The arrangement is logical, easy to use and full of helpful hints.

I believe this volume will serve a very useful purpose if carefully and thoughtfully used.

INTRODUCTION

Food allergy is a term that the medical profession is wary of, and rightly so. A great deal of press coverage has led to the popular idea that any number of foods from avocados to zucchini can cause a whole range of 'allergic' reactions including rashes, runny noses and headaches. This has meant that people have been diagnosing all sorts of food allergies for themselves and may be in danger of nutritional deficiencies by excluding too many foods from their diets.

In this book we show how a number of conditions are known to be caused by intolerance to particular foods. We and other researchers have proved by medical trials that this food intolerance can be treated by putting people on to a diet excluding the ingredients that cause their symptoms. The diets need careful balancing to ensure that they are properly nutritious and healthful, and from our menu plans and recipes you will see that they can also be made appetizing and attractive.

Unfortunately the foods that cause the conditions vary from person to person and discovering the true culprits can be time consuming and difficult. Few doctors at present have experience in this new field, so we have written this book to help people with various symptoms – and their doctors – establish whether or not they do have a food intolerance and, if so, how to deal with it.

What is allergy?

Most of the books written about food and disease call the condition 'food allergy'. Originally the word allergy meant an unpleasant reaction to any foreign substance in the body, but over the years it has changed, and now doctors use it to describe a reaction caused by a breakdown of the immune system.

The real job of the immune system is to recognize and destroy infecting agents such as bacteria and viruses that have invaded the body. Substances in the blood called antibodies are produced and these make the cells defending the body attack the germs. In allergic reactions, an abnormal type of antibody is produced that reacts to certain foreign substances called allergens, such as spores, pollens and foods. The combination of these antibodies with the allergen produces the allergic symptoms.

In most allergies doctors can detect the allergic reaction going on in the blood, but in the case of food allergy this type of reaction is hardly ever found. This is why doctors have doubted the existence of such a condition as food allergy. Yet some foods have been proved to cause disease.

How do foods produce diseases?

We are still unsure of the way that these foods cause symptoms.

We do know that some contain chemicals that upset some people but not others. Milk, for example, contains a sugar called lactose which is digested by a natural chemical called an enzyme, found in the wall of the intestine. All children have this enzyme but it disappears in all but the white races in early adult life. This means that many people develop diarrhea if they drink milk, because they are unable to break down the lactose.

We have now found that one of the reasons why some people react to chemicals is probably linked to the way the various enzymes in their bodies behave. A clue in the discovery was the action of one of the enzymes called mono-amine oxidase. Certain drugs reduce its activity, and people who are taking them have to avoid eating foods such as cheese, red wine, yeast or yeast extract, otherwise they get high blood pressure and severe headaches.

Unfortunately, it is not as simple as that – food intolerance is not always the result of the enzymes' behavior. There are other chemicals that work in different ways, including caffeine, histamine and tyramine. Caffeine is found in tea, coffee, cocoa, cola drinks and chocolate; histamine in cheese, beer, sausages and canned foods; and tyramine in brewer's yeast, red wine and cheese. Too much strong coffee produces many familiar symptoms – restlessness, palpitations, and heartburn. Histamine and tyramine may be a cause of migraine. It is thought that when they are absorbed into the body they may change the diameter of small blood vessels, and so bring on an attack in people who get migraine.

In our research in Cambridge we have found that many people who cannot eat wheat release large amounts of histamine from the lining of their intestine when wheat comes in contact with it – perhaps they have special cells there which produce this reaction.

People often develop the irritable bowel syndrome (see opposite) after a bout of gastroenteritis or repeated courses of antibiotics. We have now found that many with the condition have changes in the bacteria living in their intestines. It seems possible that these bacteria are responsible: they may break down food remnants to produce chemicals which cause the irritable bowel syndrome.

As there are so many different causes of reactions to food, and as most of them are nothing to do with allergy, you will see why we prefer to speak of 'food intolerance' rather than 'food allergy'.

Which conditions are caused by food intolerance?

As we explained, from the present state of knowledge about how foods cause disease, it can't be said that food intolerance is the cause in every case – there certainly are other known causes for all these conditions – but we and other researchers have shown by the success of our dietary treatment that food intolerance is the most common. If your child or you are diagnosed as having one of the diseases, a special diet is likely to be the remedy. But you must discuss this with your doctor, and if necessary a specialist, before you start excluding foods from your daily intake.

The conditions listed are the ones we have found are often caused by intolerance to one or other of the foods listed on page 19, and so are treated by a diet:

Irritable bowel syndrome
Migraine
Asthma
Rhinitis
Gluten-sensitive enteropathy
Eczema
Urticaria
Cow's milk sensitive enteropathy

Recently we have also had a lot of success in Cambridge treating Crohn's disease (an inflammation of the intestine) by diet, but as this is still in the experimental stages and as the disease can be severe, any change in diet should be made only under close medical supervision at a hospital specializing in the condition.

Irritable bowel syndrome

Irritable bowel syndrome is a very common condition which affects twice as many women as men; nearly one person in three in the UK suffers from it to a greater or lesser extent at one time or another. It is also often known as spastic colon. The symptoms are bad abdominal pain and distension, together with diarrhea or a very variable bowel habit. As we said earlier, people often develop symptoms after gastroenteritis or long courses of antibiotics. Yet the various x-rays and blood tests are always normal, and this has led many doctors to believe that the condition has psychological origins. People who have had abdominal pain for many years without relief tend to find life very stressful, but seeing a psychiatrist does not usually stop the symptoms, and our experience in Cambridge is that at least two-thirds of our patients suffering from irritable bowel syndrome have food intolerances. Of 182 patients treated by diet, we were able to relieve symptoms completely in 122. We wrote to eighty patients two years later to ask them how they were progressing. Seventy-one replied; fifty-nine were feeling well on their diet, and six were still well and had gone back to normal eating. So we have found treatment by diet to be far the best way of calming the irritable bowel.

Although not all cases are caused by food intolerance – menstrual changes can bring on the symptoms, and, less often, lack of fiber in the diet or short-term stress – we believe that anyone with irritable bowel syndrome should at least try an exclusion diet.

Migraine

Migraine is a very common problem, particularly in women – one woman in five between twenty and forty-five suffers from it. It has not yet been discovered why it should be so much more common in women. But migraine headaches do often run in families and usually affect only one side of the head at a time. Nausea and vomiting are associated symptoms. Attacks may last for as long as thirty-six or forty-eight hours, although many are much shorter. They seem to be brought on by a number of conditions, including fatigue, stress, excitement, fasting and bright lights as well as food.

Research carried out in the major children's hospital in London, found that of eighty-eight children who had at least one migraine a week, eighty-two were free from headaches after they had followed an exclusion diet, even when it had been thought that there were other causes. It was discovered that most of these children had a problem with four or fewer foods. Obviously it is fairly easy for children to avoid a small number of foods, and well worthwhile.

Asthma and rhinitis

Wheezing and difficulty in breathing are the main symptoms of asthma, and at night may be accompanied by coughing. There are a number of causes. It was found in one trial that some foods provoked asthma attacks in nearly 30 per cent of sufferers. Some people had only to smell the food to start an attack, although most of them actually had to eat it. Wheezing usually started an hour or two later. But food is only one cause of asthma, and as attacks can be serious, asthmatics in particular must discuss trying diet as treatment carefully with their doctors first.

Rhinitis is the medical name for a persistently runny or stuffy nose, and it can be, like asthma, related to food. Although the symptoms are so similar to a common cold, there is no confusion between the two since rhinitis doesn't come and go like a cold; it is a permanent condition. If your doctor has confirmed you have rhinitis it is certainly worth discussing trying a diet as treatment.

Gluten-sensitive enteropathy (GSE) or celiac sprue

GSE affects about one in two to three thousand people in the UK, probably one in five thousand in North America. It is a condition in which gluten, a protein found in wheat, rye and barley, damages the lining of the small intestine so that food is not properly absorbed. This leads to a number of difficulties including diarrhea, bone disease and failure to grow, or loss of weight. Anemia may also result from these problems. As the symptoms can be caused by several other conditions it is not safe to start a gluten-free diet as treatment without being diagnosed first by a specialist.

The discovery that GSE was caused by gluten was purely accidental. Most of the wheat grown in Holland during the Second

World War was directed to the German army at the Front, so the civilian population had to make do with potatoes. At this time children with GSE made dramatic improvements, and the Dutch specialist Dr W.K. Dicke made the connection, that excluding gluten from the diet had made the children better.

People with GSE recover completely once they avoid foods containing gluten but they should still be seen regularly by their specialist to make sure they are well and not lapsing on the diet, even by mistake.

Commercial gluten-free products are available, but these are useful only to people with GSE. Many of the recipes in this book are suitable for them and further help may be obtained from the national celiac society.

Eczema

Eczema is an itching red rash, often on the insides of elbows and knees, which may scale and crust. It is common in both children and adults. The rash comes and goes. It is often treated by steroid creams and antihistamine pills. Yet there is sound evidence that it can be caused by food intolerance, especially to eggs and milk. Fourteen out of twenty children tested at a children's hospital in London improved when cow's milk and eggs were taken out of their diet.

In another study at the University of Texas, thirty-two out of thirty-seven children with eczema improved after cow's milk was withdrawn from their diet and became worse when they were allowed to drink it again. The orange dye tartrazine which is found in yellow-colored food (see page 16), is also often a cause of eczema. Food reactions produce changes in the blood, which suggests people with eczema have a genuine allergy.

Urticaria

This is a very common condition, especially in children. Large red itchy blotches appear anywhere on the skin. Other symptoms are swelling of the lips and mouth. Many factors can bring on urticaria including heat, light, pressure and vibration, but in 44 per cent of children who were tested, foods, artificial dyes, preservatives and additives were the reason. More recent studies have shown that salicylates (a chemical found in aspirin and in some foods), yeasts and cow's milk are also causes.

Cow's milk sensitive enteropathy

This mainly affects babies who are bottle-fed before the age of four months. The symptoms are the severe stomach pain known as colic, diarrhea, eczema, vomiting and a runny nose. Babies usually grow out of these once they are on a solid diet, about the age of two.

Mothers who think their children are reacting to cow's milk should talk to their family doctors. Two or three simple tests (biopsies) on the small intestine while the baby is taking cow's milk and after it has been excluded show whether or not that is the trouble. Although a cow's milk-free diet may be suggested for your baby by your doctor or pediatrician, never start a child on any abnormal diet without close medical supervision.

In the next section we explain how to find a diet that will relieve you of the symptoms caused by these conditions – as long of course as food intolerance is the reason in your case. Excluding foods may be hard to start with, but the test period is relatively short, and you'll probably find there are very few foods you have to cut out for long.

The diets

If you suffer from any of the symptoms we have described, you may want to try a special diet. Discuss your symptoms beforehand with your doctor to make sure that he or she thinks this approach is sensible. You must be sure the doctor agrees that you have one of the conditions that can be treated by diet: it may be that you have another problem with similar symptoms but which needs different treatment. You should also discuss with your doctor whether or not you should continue with any pills or medicines that you may have been taking. In general, it is better to take as few pills as possible while trying these diets, as many contain starches as fillers, and they may be part of the problem.

Vegetarians should think very carefully before deciding to follow a diet which may restrict the foods available to them. Unfortunately many of the foods which most commonly produce symptoms are those that are staple items for vegetarians, such as bread, milk, cheese and eggs.

The basic principle when trying an exclusion diet is to stop eating foods that are likely to upset you and to see if your symptoms get better. Any food can produce symptoms, although some do it much more frequently than others (see the table on page 19). Taking the treatment to extremes, you would begin by eating nothing at all. This is not, of course, a practical possibility at home. In severe cases of Crohn's disease, we do stop people eating completely by feeding them with a drip until their symptoms have settled. But people with conditions such as migraine and irritable bowel syndrome are rarely ill enough to justify the great expense of this treatment.

Some doctors in the USA have advised people to live on water alone during this test period and others have suggested a diet limited to lamb and pears. We have tried these methods and now we hardly ever use them because they are both very unpleasant for the person concerned (physically and mentally) and nutritionally inadequate. Progress is slow because of the large number of foods that must be reintroduced later and if people have difficult food reactions, it takes several weeks to arrange an adequate diet. Unless your doctor specifically recommends them, extreme exclusion diets are best avoided. Never try living on water alone unless in the hospital under close supervision.

We prefer to keep our patients on broader diets, excluding only those foods which experience has shown are most likely to cause trouble. This may, of course, produce problems if people have unusual food intolerances, but it seems to work much better for most people and we have had more overall success this way.

Which diet for which condition?

Once you have discovered what your intolerances are, you should avoid only the foods that upset you. There are no reliable skin or blood tests as short cuts to discovering which foods you should avoid, and anyone with food intolerances has to work out his or her own long-term diet. However as a starting point, these are the diets we suggest for the different conditions:

Irritable bowel syndrome	Exclusion
Migraine	Exclusion
Asthma and rhinitis	Exclusion
Cow's milk sensitive enteropathy	Cow's milk-free
Gluten-sensitive enteropathy	Gluten-free
Eczema	Cow's milk and egg-free Tartrazine and salicylate-free
Urticaria	Tartrazine and salicylate-free; if this is not successful, exclusion

Every recipe in this book is marked to show which of the diets it is suitable for, and on pages 24–31 we list substitute foods you can use by themselves or in the recipes. Here are some points about the different foods you may have to exclude, depending on the condition you have.

Cow's milk   Cow's milk is one of the commonest causes of food intolerances and it is taken in many forms besides just as a drink. A list of the foods containing it is given on page 33.

We mention 'milk substitute' in many recipes. This can be soy milk, goat's or sheep's milk. Dried cow's milk, skim and sterilized milk are not suitable substitutes. Some evaporated cow's milks are said to be 'non-allergic' because they have been heated to a temperature high enough to destroy the proteins they contain. As food intolerance is not only an allergic problem, these milks are still likely to produce symptoms and so you should avoid them. The same is true of condensed milks.

Eggs   As well as not eating hens' eggs in any form, the egg-containing foods listed on page 33 have to be avoided. We don't recommend ducks' eggs as a substitute as they can contain infectious bacteria. Living on an egg-free diet may sound difficult, but there are plenty of egg-free baking recipes (and others where eggs would normally be used) in this book and they work very well.

Although there have been claims for quails' eggs, there is no scientific evidence that they are of any benefit to people with food intolerances.

Tartrazine and salicylates   Approximately one-fifth of our patients react to food additives such as preservatives and colorings. Tartrazine is a brilliant orange-yellow dye used in soft drinks and many other foods – and even in some medicines. Some foods contain salicylates which are natural chemicals similar to aspirin. Foods containing salicylates which may also cause symptoms are:

apples	liquorice
bananas	peas
beer	plums and prunes
blueberries	red wine
cider	rhubarb
grapes	strawberries

Many other additives and preservatives can cause symptoms. Manufacturers are required to list all ingredients in foods, and this includes chemicals.

Gluten and wheat   People with GSE have to exclude entirely the protein called gluten found in wheat, rye and barley, and therefore all foods containing them as well. It is important to remember that a gluten-free diet and a wheat-free diet are not exactly the same. A lot of people have an intolerance to all wheat products and not only gluten. Some commercial gluten-free flours are prepared by removing the protein from wheat flour and replacing it by a protein from other sources. The wheat starch remains, so these products must be avoided by people testing for symptoms on the exclusion diet, and those who have wheat intolerance will find that foods made from these flours still cause symptoms.

The exclusion diet

This is the diet we use to discover our patients' food intolerances, and the one we recommend you follow to establish your own. We developed it by drawing up a list of the foods that upset the 122 people in our study (see page 19) who successfully controlled their symptoms. All the foods upsetting more than 20 per cent of the patients are excluded (for the full list, see page 29).

The advantage of this diet is that it is a healthful one of fresh and wholesome foods. People often lose weight and if they are rather fussy in their likes and dislikes, they may lose a little too much. To overcome this one slight problem, we give advice on quantities to eat during the trial period on page 36.

Following an exclusion diet

This will make a bigger impression on your lifestyle and your family's than any of the other food intolerance diets. Once you realize the strict exclusion will be for only two weeks, the idea shouldn't be too discouraging. Here is a plan for following your exclusion diet:

1. For three days before starting, record all the symptoms you have had, and when, to help judge the value of the diet later on.
2. For the first two weeks keep strictly to the diet outlined on page 29. Remember it is essential to continue for two weeks; all traces of offending foods eaten before the diet began must disappear from the body before symptoms clear, and so improvement is rarely seen in the first week. Don't give up; if you take a day off you will have wasted all your previous efforts, and will have to start again from the beginning.
3. During the first two weeks it is wise to exclude any foods besides those listed on page 29 that you may suspect have upset you; later on you will test and assess them properly.
4. It is better not to smoke.
5. During the second week you should eat as wide a variety of the 'allowed' foods as possible. This will help you notice any unusual food intolerances. Some foods allowed on the exclusion diet do upset a few people. They usually find out which these are in the second week of the diet and we explain how to deal with this in 7 below.
6. Throughout the second week keep an accurate diary of every food you eat, which symptoms you have, and when. Use a small notebook and allow a spread of two pages for each day (see table on page 18).
7. You should find you steadily improve during the second week. Any unexpected setbacks at this time will probably have been caused by one of the foods eaten in the previous twenty-four hours. Compare the foods you recorded for that day with the list in the table. Any that upset 10 to 20 per cent of patients are the most likely to be the cause and if you have eaten one of these you should avoid it again until you have time to retest it.
8. If after two weeks your symptoms haven't improved, it is likely that food intolerance is not the cause of your problems. Go back to normal eating, and ask your doctor about trying other treatment.

Foods	Symptoms
Breakfast 8.00 a.m. Rice Krispies, apples, soy milk	
Mid-morning 11.15 a.m. Apple, camomile tea	Noon – diarrhea × 1
Lunch 1.30 p.m. Chicken drumsticks, chick-pea salad	
Afternoon 4.00 p.m. Water	2.30 p.m. – migraine started

Supper 8.00 p.m.
Tomato juice,
Bombay burgers,
  green salad,
    apple juice and oil dressing,
Banana	

A day from a food diary

Reintroduction

You are no doubt feeling delighted by the improvement that the diet has brought. It is now highly likely that your symptoms can be controlled by diet. However, to find out exactly which foods are responsible still requires very careful planning. Continue to keep your diary throughout the reintroduction phase. The list below shows the order for reintroduction:

1. tap water
2. potatoes
3. cow's milk
4. yeast – take 3 brewer's yeast tablets or 2 tsp baker's yeast
5. tea
6. rye – test rye crispbread and rye bread (check this is not a mixture of wheat and rye; only test rye bread if yeast was negative)
7. butter
8. onions
9. eggs
10. oats – test as oatmeal
11. coffee – test coffee beans and instant coffee separately
12. chocolate – test semi-sweet chocolate
13. barley – pearl barley, added to soups and stews
14. citrus fruits
15. corn – test cornstarch or corn on the cob
16. cow's milk cheese
17. white wine
18. shellfish
19. cow's milk yogurt – test natural yogurt, not flavored
20. vinegar

Food	Percentage of patients affected	Food	Percentage of patients affected
Cereals		*Vegetables*	
wheat	60	onions	22
corn	44	potatoes	20
oats	34	cabbage	19
rye	30	brussels sprouts	18
barley	24	peas	17
rice	15	carrots	15
		lettuce	15
		leeks	15
Dairy products		broccoli	14
milk	44	soy beans	13
cheese	39	spinach	13
eggs	26	mushrooms	12
butter	25	parsnips	12
yogurt	24	tomatoes	11
		cauliflower	11
		celery	11
Fish		green beans	10
white fish	10	cucumber	10
shellfish	10	turnip/rutabaga	10
smoked fish	7	squash	8
		beets	8
		peppers	6
Meat		*Miscellaneous*	
beef	16	coffee	33
pork	14	tea	25
chicken	13	nuts	22
lamb	11	chocolate	22
turkey	8	preservatives	20
		yeast	20
		sugar cane	13
Fruit		sugar beet	12
citrus	24	alcohol	12
rhubarb	12	saccharin	9
apples	12	honey	2
bananas	11		
pineapple	8		
pears	8		
strawberries	8		
grapes	7		
melon	5		
avocado	5		
raspberries	4		

Foods tested by patients attending our clinic

21. wheat – test as whole-wheat bread; white bread can be tested later; if yeast upsets you, test wheat as wheatflakes
Note: Wheat produces its effects slowly, so test for twice as long as other foods
22. nuts
23. preservatives – soft drinks, canned foods, mono-sodium glutamate (MSG), saccharin

How you begin reintroducing these foods depends on which condition you have. For migraine, irritable bowel syndrome, asthma and rhinitis we believe that one food should be reintroduced every two days. For eczema and urticaria a longer period of a week may be necessary. One method of testing is to use a rotating diet. We have not found this satisfactory as it quite often takes twenty-four to forty-eight hours for a reaction to a food to show, and on a rotating diet this leads to confusion about which food is responsible. Here are the rules to follow for reintroduction:

● If you have a reaction, stop eating the food you are testing immediately or you may suffer severe symptoms; do not continue testing new foods until you are completely well again. In any case, follow these instructions carefully and don't try to rush – the more haste, the less speed. The average reintroduction time for people we see is two months, with four visits to our clinic.

● The time it takes for symptoms to show also varies. Do not expect it always to be immediately after eating a food. Sometimes they appear so slowly that they are hardly noticeable. This is why it is so important to keep a diary – you can look back and see when you were last really well and this will help you spot the offending food.

● Eat plenty of the food you are testing – at least two good helpings a day. If after the last test day there are no ill-effects, you may assume that the food is safe to eat in normal quantities, and use in cooking.

● Some foods (for example bread and wine) are made up of more than one ingredient. Test the ingredient concerned before trying the food: for example, test yeast before bread or wine; otherwise, if a reaction occurs, you will not know which ingredient caused it.

● It is wise to leave the testing of wheat until late in the reintroduction as this is the most common cause of problems, and it is better to try it with a little experience under your belt.

● Flush out the chemicals in your system produced by the food reaction by drinking plenty of water. Some people find that adding a little baking soda increases the effectiveness of this treatment. And don't forget, don't take pills to relieve any symptoms, for they confuse matters. Aspirin, for example, contains wheat and cornstarches.

● Sometimes you may suspect that a food upsets you, but are not absolutely sure. Don't waste time testing and retesting one food; omit it for two or three weeks and come back to it later when your diet is less restricted.

● At the end of the reintroduction you must go back and retest all foods you believe affect you. Some suspected reactions may have been coincidence and some food intolerances rapidly disappear. There is no point in avoiding a food unless you really have to.

● When you have finished your testing and identified all the foods which upset you, ask your doctor to arrange a visit to a dietitian to check that the diet you are planning to follow is nutritious.

● Unfortunately this reintroduction may not be final. Intolerances can change: operations, courses of antibiotics, virus infections and bouts of gastroenteritis are some of the reasons for this happening; it may be easy for you to identify a food that has brought back your symptoms, but if you are unlucky, you may have to go through the testing again at any time in the future.

Will you be able to eat the upsetting foods again?
A reliable way to rid people of their intolerances has not yet been found. Several methods have been tried such as taking drops under the tongue, enzyme desensitization which involves putting drops on the skin, and various drugs, but they are still in the experimental stage and we have found all of them disappointing.

While the intolerance continues, you will have to resign yourself to excluding the upsetting foods – as long as that seems preferable to suffering from the symptoms.

However, many people find that after avoiding a food for some months, it no longer upsets them, so recheck your food intolerances periodically – say every six months – and you may be pleasantly surprised. Celiacs must of course always stick to their diet to avoid serious damage to the small intestine.

What should you do if you have many food intolerances?
If you are unlucky and find a large number of foods upset you, you should think seriously about whether it's worth trying to control your symptoms by diet, and you should certainly ask a dietitian to

check the nutritional value of what you are eating and discuss other ways of coping with your symptoms with your doctor. If he or she feels that you can go on controlling your symptoms by diet rather than with drugs, it may help if you rotate your diet. We have found that when people can safely eat only a few foods, they eat so much of them that they may later have trouble with these foods as well. Rotating your diet means that you eat foods from each food family only every four or five days, so that you are not overexposed to any (food families are given on page 31).

Here is a suggested rotating diet; obviously you will have to adapt it according to your particular intolerances.

Day 1	**Day 2**	**Day 3**	**Day 4**
rice	potatoes	millet	buckwheat groats
poultry	lamb	fish	beef
carrots	tomatoes	broccoli	green beans
melon	pineapple	bananas	apples

Good nutrition on the exclusion diet

Energy One of the main problems with the first stage of the exclusion diet is the provision of adequate energy or calories. As potatoes and bread are not allowed, many people find it difficult to eat enough starchy carbohydrates to maintain their weight. Weight loss and hunger are very common when following this diet, and you should try to avoid them. Rice, millet and buckwheat with root vegetables such as parsnips, rutabagas and turnips are good substitutes. As well as containing calories, they give us protein, minerals and vitamins. We recommend the use of brown rice as this is more nutritious and contains more fiber than the highly refined white rice.

Recipes are also given for cookies, cakes and desserts, which will help to fill you up. These should be used in moderation unless you find difficulty in keeping your weight steady. If you are overweight before starting the diet then do not use these sugary foods. Now is the time to lose those unhealthy extra pounds!

Fiber With the exclusion of cereals such as wheat, rye and oats the fiber content of the diet will be lowered; fiber is of course very effective, not only in avoiding constipation, but many other bowel disorders. You should ensure your fiber intake is sufficient by eating plenty of brown rice, millet, buckwheat, fruit and vegetables. Legumes (such as kidney, soy and navy beans) are particularly good sources of fiber. Aim to include at least 30g/1oz of fiber a day. To increase your fiber intake, soy and rice bran can be bought from a health food shop or drug store. If constipation becomes a problem despite these additions to the diet, buy a bulk laxative from your drug store. These laxatives are made from the husks of plant seeds– a harmless form of roughage which has been used to help bowel conditions for many years in Eastern countries and very rarely upsets people with food intolerances.

Vitamins and minerals As long as you eat widely on the exclusion diet, you should avoid deficiencies. If, however, you are cow's milk intolerant and not using a milk substitute, calcium may be lacking and so supplements may be necessary. Calcium is available in other foods; alternatively you can take it in pills. Calcium lactate and gluconate are easily available from drug stores.

If you have become anemic because of your condition, or you are intolerant of many iron-containing foods, you will need iron supplements. The best form is the ferrous sulfate mixture used for children, which has few ingredients. Your doctor can supply this.

You should be very careful about taking extra vitamins, especially fat-soluble ones (A,D,E,K) as this can be dangerous, and the cult of 'megavitamins' has already led to people poisoning themselves in the US. However, a small additional supplement of B vitamins often helps people on the exclusion diet, especially if they feel tired. Many vitamin pills are now produced free of wheat starch– check this with your doctor or drug store. A suitable daily vitamin B supplement would be:

Thiamine hydrochloride	150 mg
Riboflavin	15 mg
Nicotinamide	600 mg
Pyridoxine	100 mg
Ascorbic acid (vitamin C)	300 mg daily could be added to this

The best source of vitamin D is sunshine on the bare skin. Get out and about as often as you can, especially on sunny days. A vacation in the sun is of tremendous benefit.

Enjoying your food

If you find that you have food intolerances, you cannot expect your diet to be just the same as ever, any more than you expect the food to be the same abroad as at home. You have to be willing to experiment a little and get used to new tastes and textures. Most people's eating habits have to fit in with their families and friends, so we have tried to include dishes that they will enjoy too. Old favorites such as roast beef are fine, and can be easily adapted to suit your diet. There are substitutes for all the common ingredients such as wheat products and cow's milk, and we show here how you can use them in your cooking.

Grains and flours

The gluten in flours used for baking is elastic and holds air. This is why a strong (high-gluten) wheat flour is ideal for breadmaking. Grains suitable for celiacs or people with wheat intolerance are less likely to rise and great patience is needed to master the skills of breadmaking with gluten-free flours (we give advice on page 88).

Most of the flours listed are obtainable from health food shops, some supermarkets and mail-order sources, or may be milled from the grains in a powerful domestic blender.

Arrowroot is a starchy root with the consistency of cornstarch. It is almost pure starch, providing little besides carbohydrate and is most useful as a thickening agent for gravies and sauces.

Another exotic thickener is *kuzu* from Japan.

Buckwheat is confusingly named as it comes from plants of the same family as dock leaves and so is all right for people with wheat intolerance. The flour, which has a strong and distinctive flavor, has an egg-like binding capacity which makes it very good in batters. It contains some protein and is rich in B vitamins. Some buckwheat products (for example, spaghetti) are sold ready-made. Read the labels with special care as many also contain wheat flour.

Carob flour is ground from the pod of the locust tree and has a strong chocolate taste. As well as being high in pectin, it contains appreciable amounts of proteins, carbohydrates, calcium and phosphorus. It is an invaluable alternative to chocolate for flavoring cakes and drinks.

Chestnut flour is derived from the sweet chestnut. It does have a distinctive flavor and is rather heavy, but can be used for baking cakes and cookies (for example, shortbread, scones, fruit crumbles or crisps).

Chickpea flour is made from ground legumes. It is widely used in Indian breads and batters and, like soy flour, is high in protein, vitamins and minerals. It has a strong flavor and will go bitter if kept too long.

Corn meal is a good thickening agent. It may be used in baking cakes, cookies and bread, or for the Italian dish, *polenta* (similar to oatmeal or hominy grits, but eaten as a luncheon or dinner dish.

Millet, like rice, is a member of the grass family, but both are distant enough relatives of wheat to be safe for many people with wheat intolerance. It has good nutritional value, providing B vitamins, minerals and proteins. Millet is available as a grain, a flake or a flour. It can be used in a variety of sweet and main courses as it is filling and pleasant-tasting.

Potato flour, sometimes called *fécule* or *farina*, is an excellent thickening agent and useful for baking. It is a pure starch with little flavor of its own. (Note: Instant mashed potato contains chemical additives and is not a substitute for pure potato flour.)

Rice. Brown rice is preferable to white as it contains many vitamins (especially group B) as well as minerals and fiber.

Rice flour, rice flakes and ground rice can be used in baking cookies and making desserts. Rice flour is best mixed with other flours as it has a strong flavor.

Sago flour is like rice flour in texture but comes from the trunk of the palm tree. It is good for desserts, and thickening stews, and has no strong flavor.

Soy flour is made from ground soybeans. It is an excellent source of protein, fat and B vitamins. It has a strong flavor and is best used in combination with other dishes, where it increases the protein value.

Tapioca comes from the root of a tropical plant (cassava). Like sago it is almost pure starch. It is used by itself to make a pudding, but is also handy for thickening soups and stews.

Cooking grains

Brown rice   Wash and drain the rice. Allow twice the volume of cooking water to rice. Bring the water to a boil, add rice and ½ to 1 tsp salt, depending on quantity being cooked. Turn heat down, cover and simmer for about 40 minutes until tender and the water is absorbed. Do not stir the rice while it is cooking as this breaks up the grains. Fluff with a fork when done.

Buckwheat   This grain can be bought either roasted or unroasted, the roasted being rather stronger in flavor. The type you choose depends on your preference. Place the buckwheat into twice its volume of cold salted water, bring to a boil and simmer until all the moisture has been absorbed and the buckwheat is soft (about 15 minutes). Unroasted buckwheat takes slightly longer to cook than roasted. Do not stir while cooking.

Millet   Cook as for buckwheat. In some dishes millet can be dry-roasted in the pan first to enhance the flavor.

Dairy products

Cheese   A large number of excellent cheeses made from goat's or ewe's milk are available. These are listed on page 31. There is also a cheese made from soy milk.

Cooking fats As a cow's milk product, butter is not allowed. In most recipes we have used Kosher margarine as it is easily available in large supermarkets and health food stores, and milk-free. In North America, similar margarines made entirely from vegetable products can be used.

Lard is derived from animal fats and so is unlikely to cause problems to most people with milk intolerance. Those who prefer to cook with polyunsaturated fats may use oils such as safflower or sunflower. Commercial 'vegetable oil' is a blend and usually contains corn oil.

Ewe's milk is not a widely available product but you may find it in some country localities. It is certainly worth trying, although we have no personal experience of its use. We do have reports that sheep's milk yogurt is very palatable.

Goat's milk is widely available from health food stores and some supermarkets, but you need to be reassured about its source. Goat's milk is not pasteurized, and sometimes carries salmonella, but very rarely TB or brucellosis. Home pasteurization is impractical, but boiling the milk is useful. Goat's milk can be stored in the refrigerator or deep frozen (many people prefer to drink it chilled).

The value of goat's milk is limited. People whose asthma, hayfever or eczema are caused by cow's milk and who have switched to goat's milk often find that they then become intolerant to this. Similarly, some people with irritable bowel syndrome have found goat's milk only a temporary help.

Soy milk is made from soybeans and may be obtained from health food shops. Unopened, it keeps without refrigeration but should be kept in the refrigerator for no more than three days after opening. Commercially produced soy milk doesn't have a strong flavor and it can be used in cooking as an alternative to cow's milk. Some brands contain cane sugar, sea salt and sunflower oil to enhance the flavor. You can make your own soy milk from soy flour:

Soy milk
Makes approximately 1 l/1 quart

150 g/1¼ cups soy flour
Vanilla bean, honey or concentrated apple juice (optional)

Mix flour with 1 l/3¾ cups water in a saucepan. Bring slowly to a boil, stirring all the time. (Caution! This mixture quickly froths over like cow's milk when boiling.) Reduce the heat and simmer for 20 minutes, stirring frequently.

The milk can be flavored with honey, apple juice or vanilla bean. Add apple juice when the milk has cooled, otherwise it curdles.

Use as a milk substitute. Store in the refrigerator as it ferments when exposed to heat.

Savory flavorings

Miso is a fermented mixture of cereal grains, soybeans, water and salt. The form containing rice will be suitable for many with food intolerance, but be careful not to confuse this with other varieties containing wheat or barley. Miso is rich in protein, minerals and vitamins, including vitamin B_{12}. It has a thick, pasty consistency and is thinned with water (but not boiling as this curdles it) to be used as a stock base in soups, stews, sauces and gravies.

Tahini This is made from sesame seeds crushed and blended with oil. It is useful for making sauces and in the dip, hummus. For people who can't tolerate lemon, an added amount of garlic and parsley makes an excellent alternative. Tahini can also be included in salad dressing or used as a sandwich spread.

Drinks

Hot carob-flavoured soy milk is relaxing at bedtime (use the carob flour like cocoa). Earlier in the day, pineapple juice is refreshing. Herbal teas, maté and chicory are handy. Some teas come in individual tea-bags which are useful to take to work. Ground chicory can be brewed in the same way as ground coffee. Try apple juice, or grape and apple juice mix, with ice and a sprig of mint, or tomato juice with a touch of paprika. These are sophisticated enough to drink in the early evening, and you can become quite a connoisseur of mineral water with your dinner.

Some mineral waters are still, some naturally sparkling and some artificially carbonated and described as sparkling. Many supermarkets' own brands fall into this category, and are very gassy. Perrier has a small mineral content and strong effervescence. Badiot from St Galmer in the Loire produces a softly sparkling water with medium mineral content. Vichy-Celestin is another natural sparkler: it has a higher mineral content than Badiot. A particularly flavored mineral water with a very high mineral content is St-Yorre, which sparkles and has a strong salty alkaline taste. Delicious still waters abound in many regions of North America.

Shopping: foods to buy and foods to avoid

On the following pages we list some of the less well-known fresh fruits and vegetables normally acceptable to people with food intolerances, and suggest ways of cooking them as they introduce as much variety as possible into a restricted diet. We also list the foods, especially processed foods, that you should avoid, at least on the first part of the exclusion diet. Armed with this information, you should not find shopping for your special diet too confusing or discouraging.

Always buy fresh or frozen foods. Ingredients in canned and packaged foods should be checked for food additives, which must be avoided as far as possible. The table opposite is a general guide to categories of allowed and not-allowed foods during the first two weeks of the exclusion diet. For more detailed information on the latter, see pages 33–5.

Vegetables

Celeriac has a mild celery flavor. Add chopped to soups or casseroles or cook and serve puréed with game. Very good grated raw in salads. Another way of serving is to peel, shred and blanch the celeriac and mix with mayonnaise, garlic and mustard.

Fennel has a crunchy texture with a mild aniseed flavor. Serve raw, shredded in salads or boil until tender and serve with white sauce. Excellent with fish. The feathery leaves can be used to flavor salads.

Okra (ladies' fingers) are soft and have a syrupy texture. Trim each pod and boil for five minutes. Delicious with curries or a tomato sauce.

Plantain tastes like banana but is less sweet. It is always eaten cooked. Peel, boil and mash, or bake whole in its skin.

Pumpkin has a juicy, delicate flavor. Remove the skin, pith and seeds. Cut flesh into small chunks and boil for ten minutes, or steam. Serve with cheese sauce. Can also be used in curries, soups or sweet desserts.

Salsify (oyster plant) has a flavor similar to Jerusalem artichokes. Peel and boil in salted water with a few drops of lemon juice (if allowed) until tender. Cut into pieces and serve with melted vegetable margarine, lemon juice and herbs, or with a cheese sauce. Alternatively chop and fry in vegetable margarine until deep golden brown and serve with a squeeze of lemon juice.

Snow peas have a sweet and crisp flavor. Trim, then boil for 1–2 minutes. Serve tossed in vegetable margarine. Can also be served raw, finely sliced in salads.

Sweet potatoes can be substituted for potatoes. Can be boiled, baked or steamed. If boiled, add a little lemon juice to the water to prevent discoloration (provided it is allowed). Very good mashed and flavored with cinnamon, nutmeg or orange.

Water chestnuts have a delicate, juicy flavor, with a crisp nutty texture. Wash and peel carefully. Add raw to salads, toast or stir fry.

Yams Substitute for potatoes. They have a faint nutty flavor. Cook and serve as for sweet potatoes.

Foods for the exclusion diet

	Not allowed	Allowed
Meat	preserved meats, bacon, sausages	all other meats
Fish	smoked fish, shellfish	white fish
Vegetables	potatoes, onions, corn on the cob	all other vegetables and salads, legumes, rutabaga, parsnip
Fruit	citrus fruit, eg, oranges, grapefruit	all other fruit, eg, apples, bananas, pears
Cereals	wheat (see page 33), oats, barley, rye, corn (see page 35)	rice, ground rice, rice flakes, rice flour, sago, Rice Krispies, tapioca, millet, buckwheat, rice cakes
Cooking oils	corn oil, vegetable oil	sunflower oil, soy oil, safflower oil, olive oil
Dairy products	cow's milk (see page 33), butter, most margarines, cow's milk, yogurt and cheese, eggs	goat's milk, soy milk, sheep's milk, Kosher margarine, goat's and sheep's milk yogurt and cheese
Beverages	tea, coffee – beans, instant and decaffeinated, soft drinks, orange juice, grapefruit juice, alcohol, tap water	herbal teas, eg, camomile, fresh fruit juices, eg, apple, pineapple, tomato juice, mineral, distilled or deionized water
Miscellaneous	chocolates, yeast (see page 34), preservatives	carob, sea salt, herbs, spices, in moderation: sugar, honey

Note: Some fruits, especially overripe ones, contain small amounts of yeast but the quantities rarely cause any problems.

Fruits

Guava has a firm milky texture and a faint strawberry flavor. Peel and eat alone or with fruit salad. Use for sherbert and for making jam and jelly.

Kiwi fruit have a delicious sharp taste. Peel and slice thinly into fruit or vegetable salads.

Lychees have the texture of a grape. Peel and eat.

Mango has a sweet and slightly gingery flavor. Remove skin and pit. Use in fruit salads, ice cream, sherbert and for making chutneys.

Suggestions for vegetable combinations

First vegetable	How cooked	Second vegetable	How cooked	Combine and serve
brussels sprouts	boiled in salted water	sweet chestnuts	peeled and fried in Kosher margarine for 2 minutes	add sprouts to Kosher margarine and nut mixture, stir and fry a further few minutes
carrot, grated	fried in Kosher margarine	chopped chicory heads, chopped bean sprouts	fried for the last 5 minutes	Stir in apple juice for last minute of frying and season
celery	stalks, 4 cm/1½ in long, ½ cm/¼ in wide, lightly boiled	walnut pieces	fried in Kosher margarine	add celery to margarine and nut mixture, stir and fry an additional few minutes
green beans	fried in Kosher margarine with mixed herbs	crisp lettuce	added to beans for last 5 minutes	hot, immediately
leeks, washed and cut into 3 cm/1 in long pieces	boiled in salted water	skinned and chopped tomatoes	fried in oil with slices of garlic	pour tomatoes over chopped leeks, garnish with chopped parsley
pole beans	boiled in salted water	finely chopped celery, skinned, chopped tomatoes	fried in garlic and oil	stir yogurt into cooked celery and tomato mixture, add concentrated tomato paste; serve on beans garnished with chopped parsley
red cabbage	shredded and boiled 5–10 minutes with a few caraway seeds	red pepper	fried in oil for 1 minute with cabbage	hot, immediately
spinach	boiled in very little salted water	celery	chopped and fried in oil	season and stir spinach into celery, fry an additional few minutes
spinach	boiled in very little lightly salted water	goat's yogurt	stir in crushed garlic and season	mix together well and serve hot
zucchini	sliced and simmered with mint and peas for 5–6 minutes	peas	simmered with mint and zucchini	toss in melted Kosher margarine with chopped chives

Passion fruit has a sweet, seedy pulp. Remove top and scoop out flesh. Eat alone or add to fruit salads.

Papaya is similar to a melon, with a faint scented flavor. Slice in half, remove black seeds and eat raw, sprinkled with lemon juice if allowed.

Physalis is a tart citrus berry. Remove husk, eat raw or use in pies or tarts.

Sharon fruit is a seedless persimmon tasting like a sweet peach. Slice into fruit salads or blend with ice cream.

French cheeses made with sheep's or goat's milk
Cheeses marked with an asterisk are the most easily obtainable. The others are likely to be found only in their own area of production.

Cheese	Type of milk
Arnéguy	sheep's
Asco	goat's
Bougon*	goat's
Bouton-de-Culotte	goat's
Chabichou*	goat's
Chevrotin*	goat's
Chevrotin persillé des Aravis*	goat's
Crottin de Chavignol*	goat's
Iraty	sheep's
Laruns	sheep's
Levroux	goat's
Macon	goat's
Pélardon	goat's
Picodon	goat's
Pouligny-Saint-Pierre	goat's
Pyramide*	goat's
Roquefort*	sheep's
Ruffec	goat's
Saint-Foy	goat's
Saint-Maixent	goat's
Saint-Maure	goat's
Sancerre	goat's
Selle-sur-Cher	goat's
Tome d'Arles*	sheep's
Valençay	goat's

Food families
It is useful to know which family particular foods belong to since intolerance to one may mean that other members of the group cause symptoms.

Plants

Caricaceae: papaya
Chenopodiaceae: beets, spinach, sugar beet
Compositae: artichokes (globe and Jerusalem), camomile, chicory, endive, lettuce, safflower, salsify, sunflower, tarragon
Convolvulaceae: sweet potato
Cruciferae: bok choy, broccoli, Brussels sprouts, cabbage, cauliflower, horseradish, kale, kohlrabi, mustard, rape, rutabaga, turnip, watercress
Cucurbitaceae: cucumber, melon, pumpkin, squash, zucchini
Cycadaceae: sago
Dioscoreaceae: yam
Ebenaceae: persimmon
Ericaceae: blueberry, cranberry
Euphorbiaceae: cassava, tapioca
Fungi: mushrooms
Gramineae: barley, corn, millet, oats, rice, rye, sugar cane, wheat
Labiatae: balm, basil, marjoram, mint, oregano, peppermint, rosemary, sage
Leguminosae: dry beans, green beans, lentils, liquorice, peanuts, peas
Liliaceae: asparagus, chives, garlic, leek, onion
Malvaceae: okra
Marantaceae: arrowroot
Moraceae: mulberry
Musaceae: banana, plantain
Myrtaceae: guava
Onagraceae: water chestnut
Palmae: coconut, dates
Passifloraceae: passion fruit
Polygonaceae: buckwheat, rhubarb
Rosaceae: apple, apricot, blackberry, cherry, loganberry, nectarine, peach, pear, plum, prune, raspberry, strawberry,
Rubiaceae: coffee
Rutaceae: grapefruit, lemon, lime, mandarin orange, orange, tangerine
Saxifragaceae: black and red currants, gooseberry
Solanaceae: cayenne, eggplant, paprika, pepper, physalis, potato, tobacco, tomato
Theaceae: tea
Umbelliferae: angelica, caraway, carrots, celeriac, celery, coriander, dill, fennel, parsley, parsnips, samphire (glasswort)
Vitaceae: grape, vine

Animal

Dairy products: butter, cheese, milk, yogurt

Crustaceans: crab, crayfish, lobster, shrimp
Molluscs: clam, mussel, oyster, scallop, snail, squid

Food containing cow's milk and cow's milk products

Milk is used in a variety of manufactured products. Check all
labels on commercially bought foods and if the following items
are contained, do not use that product: milk, butter, margarine,
cream, cheese, yogurt, skim milk powder, nonfat milk solids,
caseinates, whey, lactalbumin, lactose.

The foods listed below are likely to contain milk and/or milk
products, so always check the list of ingredients:

bread, bread mixes
breakfast cereals
cakes, cake mixes
candies, eg, milk chocolate, fudge, toffee
convenience foods: fish, meat, rice and pasta dishes
cookies
gravy mixes
malted milk drinks, eg, Ovaltine
puddings and mixes, ice cream, junket, custards
sauces, cream soups
sausages
vegetables canned in sauce

Foods containing eggs

Foods containing egg yolk, egg white, and lecithin should be
avoided. The following may contain eggs:

baked foods – cakes, cookies, pastry and batter
dessert mixes
egg noodles and pasta
lemon curd
malted milk drink, eg, Ovaltine
mayonnaise ·
soups

Foods containing wheat

Wheat is present in the following products. Check all labels on
manufactured foods. If wheat, wheat starch, edible starch, cereal
filler, cereal binder or cereal protein are listed in the ingredients
do not use that product. Foods marked with an asterisk may or
may not contain wheat.

Beverages: cocoa,* hot chocolate,* coffee extract,* milk shake
flavorings,* Ovaltine,*
Bread: including white, wholewheat, granary breads, rye bread,*
low-calorie bread

Breakfast cereals, eg, Shredded Wheat, Puffed Wheat, All-Bran, muesli,* Grapenuts, baby cereals*

Cakes: including homemade and purchased cakes, cake mixes and scones

Cookies: homemade and purchased

Dairy products and fats: cheese spreads,* processed cheese,* packaged suet*

Fish: canned,* fish paste,* fish cooked in batter, bread crumbs or a sauce

Flours and cereals: ordinary wheat flours, bran, wheat germ, semolina, pasta, noodles

Fruit: pie fillings*

Meat: canned,* convenience foods,* meat pies, sausage rolls, meat paste,* pâté,* sausages*

Pastry: homemade, purchased, mixes and frozen

Puddings and desserts: packaged puddings, dessert mixes,* ice cream,* mousse,* custard powder*

Soups: canned and packaged

Vegetables: canned in sauces, eg, baked beans,* canned vegetable salad,* instant mashed potato*

Miscellaneous: stuffings, savory spreads,* mayonnaise,* curry powder,* mustard,* chutney,* mincemeat,* peanut butter,* lemon curd,* candy and chocolates,* baking powder,* gravy mixes,* bouillon cubes,* soy sauce,* pepper compounds, packaged seasonings

Foods containing yeast
The following products can, and frequently do, contain yeast in one form or another.

Bread: any kind of bread, except soda bread, bread pudding, stuffings made with bread crumbs, bread crumb coatings on, eg, fish fingers, fish cakes, potato croquettes

Buns made with yeast eg, coffee cake, danish, rolls, crumpets, doughnuts

Cheese, yogurt, buttermilk, sour cream, synthetic cream

Fermented beverages, eg, wine, beer, cider

Fruit juice (home-squeezed citrus fruits are yeast-free)

Grapes, golden raisins, currants, plums, dates, prunes and products containing these, eg, fruit cake, mincemeat, muesli, raisin bran

Malted milk drinks, eg, Ovaltine

Meat products containing bread, eg, sausages,* meat loaf, beefburgers*

Overripe fruit

Pizza

Puddings made with bread, eg, apple charlotte, bread pudding, summer pudding

Vinegar and pickled foods, eg, pickled onions, pickled beets, sauces containing vinegar, eg, tomato catsup, salad dressing, mayonnaise

Vitamin products: most B vitamin products contain yeast

Yeast extract, Bovril, most bouillon cubes and gravy mixes, canned and packaged soups

Foods containing corn

The products listed can and frequently do contain corn in one form or another, as cornstarch, oil, syrup or cornmeal. Edible starch, food starch, corn oil, glucose syrup, vegetable oil and dextrose are also usually derived from corn. Always check the label of manufactured products. Products marked with an asterisk may or may not contain corn.

Baking mixtures for cakes and cookies*
Baking powders*
Bleached white flour
Bottled sauces – many contain food starch or syrup*
Cakes and cookies*
Canned foods, eg, soups, puddings, baked beans*
Cornflakes
Cornstarch
Custard powder
Gravy mixes
Ices, ice creams*
Instant puddings*
Instant teas, eg, lemon tea mix contains dextrose
Jams, jellies*
Margarine and vegetable oils containing corn oil
Peanut butter*
Polenta
Popcorn
Salad dressings*
Sweets – may be sweetened with corn syrup, eg, sherberts, marshmallows
Tortillas

Sample menus

These are rough guides to the amount of food which should be eaten when following the first stage of the exclusion diet. They are worked out for men and women of ideal weight. If you are over-weight, cut down on both fats and sugars. Do not fry foods, use only a scraping of vegetable margarine on biscuits and do not use it on vegetables. Do not eat sugary foods such as cakes and high-calorie desserts. It is important, however, to maintain a sufficient fiber intake, so eat plenty of starchy foods high in fiber, for example, brown rice, buckwheat groats, fruits and vegetables.

If you are underweight, try eating snacks between meals. Recipes are given for crackers, cookies and cakes which you may find useful. Increase the amount of milk substitute to 600 ml/2½ cups a day. Milk drinks such as carob milk are very tasty. If your appetite is good you can also have larger main courses. More meat, fish, vegetables and rice can be taken. Dessert will also help provide extra calories.

Meal plan for adults of ideal weight
The foods and quantities given below can be eaten by anyone using this book. Extra recommendations for men are given in brackets.

Daily: 275–425 ml/1⅛–1¾ cups milk substitute [425 ml/1¾ cups]

Breakfast
Fruit juice
30 g/1 cup Rice Krispies with milk substitute
2 buckwheat and rice crackers with Kosher margarine [4]
2 portions fruit, eg, apple, banana

Lunch
Fruit juice
100 g/3½ oz meat or 150 g/5 oz fish
large helping vegetables or salad
90 g/½ cup brown rice, buckwheat or millet [120 g/⅝ cup]
2 portions fruit [2 crackers with Kosher margarine in addition]

Supper
Fruit juice
100 g/3½ oz meat or 150 g/5 oz fish
large helping vegetables or salad
90 g/½ cup brown rice, buckwheat or millet [120 g/⅝ cup]
Dessert, eg, milk pudding made with sago

Bedtime
Fruit juice
2 portions fruit

Suggested menus: Exclusion diet

Breakfast
Apple juice
Muesli and milk substitute
Buckwheat and rice crackers with Kosher margarine

Lunch
Spiced apple juice
Stuffed tomatoes
Green salad
Anytime-of-year fruit salad with sheep's yogurt

Supper
Fruit cocktail
Celeriac soup
Rosemary and garlic lamb
Millet
Carrots
Apricot mold

Bedtime
Carob milk drink

Wheat-free diet

Breakfast
Fruit juice
Millet flake granola and milk
Buckwheat brown bread and butter with marmalade

Lunch
Pizza
Mixed salad
Dried fruit compote

Supper
Melon and grape savory appetizer
Balkan chops
Green beans
Baked potatoes
Fruit tart

Milk-free diet

Breakfast
Fruit juice
Millet flake granola with milk substitute
Toast, Kosher margarine, marmalade

Lunch
Savory buckwheat pancakes
Mixed salad
Baked bananas and nut cream

Supper
Chestnut soup and wholewheat rolls

Turkey with apple and cherries
Carrots
Potatoes
Summer fruit dessert

Egg-free diet

Breakfast
Fruit juice
Muesli and milk
Broiled bacon and tomato
Wholewheat bread, butter and brewer's yeast

Lunch
Chicken Waldorf
Savory rice
Stuffed baked apples

Supper
Four-meat pâté with white toast
Crispy coated fish
Creamed spinach
Potatoes
Peach condé

THE RECIPES

All the recipes in this book are as far as possible free from artificial colorings, flavorings and preservatives. They are also free from gluten (wheat, rye and barley), other wheat, corn, oats and cow's milk. If you simply want to exclude one or more of these from your diet you may choose any recipe you wish. If you are following the first stage of the exclusion diet or are excluding eggs, you should select only those appropriately marked. If other foods are to be excluded you will need to examine the list of ingredients in each recipe carefully to see whether it is suitable for your diet.

Where you are advised to use a milk substitute, use any that is suitable for you, such as goat's, sheep's or soy milk.

Symbols
The symbols used in this book for the specials diets are:

✱	exclusion
W	wheat-free
M	milk-free
E	egg-free

Measurements
The measurements are given in both metric and lb/cup/spoon units. Use one system only; do not combine them.

Where spoonfuls are referred to, level spoons are meant unless otherwise stated.

1 tsp (teaspoon) = 5 ml
1 tbsp (tablespoon) = 15 ml

To ensure success, check the size of the utensils you are using. Standard measuring spoons and cups eliminate guesswork.

BREAKFASTS

Muesli   ⋆ W M E

Serves 6

*170 g/1 cup buckwheat or millet
or 225 g/1⅛ cups brown rice*

*120 g/⅔ cup dried fruit (eg, apricots,
peaches, raisins)
30 ml/2 tbsp honey if desired*

Cook the buckwheat, millet or rice according to instructions (see page 25). Cool. Mix with chopped dried fruit. Honey can be added to sweeten the muesli.
Serve with milk substitute.

Millet flake granola   W M E

Makes 565 g/1¼ lb granola

*225 g/2¼ cups millet flakes
120 g/1 cup nuts (mixed flaked
almonds, chopped filberts)*

*8 tbsp honey
15 ml/1 tbsp oil
120 g/⅔ cup raisins*

Preheat oven to 350 °F/180 °C.
Mix millet flakes, nuts, honey and oil together. Spread mixture thinly over 2 baking sheets.
Bake for 30 minutes, turning occasionally so that the millet is evenly and lightly browned.
Cool the granola. Mix in the raisins.
Store in a sealed jar for up to 1 month.
Serve as a breakfast cereal with milk or on top of yogurt or fruit as a dessert.

Buckwheat breakfast   W M

Serves 4

*4 buckwheat pancakes (see page 45)
tomatoes, sliced*   *sugar, salt, pepper, mixed herbs*

Cook pancakes according to instructions.
Broil tomato slices lightly sprinkled with sugar, salt, pepper and mixed herbs for 1–2 minutes until just cooked.
Place on pancakes and serve.

Milk shake (*top*, see page 46), Millet flake granola (*center*), Buckwheat breakfast (*bottom*). OVERLEAF: Melon and grape savory appetizer (*top left*, see page 48), Fruit cocktail (*top right*, see page 47), Spinach roulade (*bottom left*, see page 49), Cocktail nibbles (*bottom right*, see page 48)

Hot fruity breakfast ☒ W M E

Serves 1

30 g/2 tbsp lightly crushed millet,
   toasted
120 ml/½ cup milk substitute

stewed fruit (gooseberries are good,
   fresh or bottled)
golden syrup (optional)

Mix the millet and milk in a pan, bring gently to a boil and simmer for 5 minutes, stirring occasionally.

Place in serving bowl, stir in 1–2 tbsp stewed fruit, and serve with extra milk substitute or a luxurious blob of golden syrup.

Buckwheat pancakes ☒ W M E

Serves 4

(1)

60 g/⅝ cup buckwheat flour
60 g/½ cup rice flour
15 g/1 tbsp Kosher margarine, melted
   in a saucepan, or 30 ml/1 tbsp of
   oil

⅛ tsp sea salt
1 tsp commercial wheat-free baking
   powder (see page 89)
300 ml/1¼ cups milk substitute

Sift the flours and salt together. Mix with melted margarine or oil and milk substitute and beat well. Leave to stand for 30 minutes before using. Just before using stir in the baking powder.

To make the pancakes, put about ⅔ tbsp oil into a frying pan and heat until just beginning to smoke. Quickly pour in enough batter to coat the base of the pan thinly and tilt the pan to make sure that the batter runs evenly all over. Let the pancake set and brown underneath, then turn it gently with a spatula – do not toss the pancake – and brown it on the other side.

Serve with savory or sweet fillings.

(2) W M

60 g/⅝ cup buckwheat flour
60 g/½ cup rice flour
⅛ tsp salt

1 egg
300 ml/1¼ cups milk substitute

Sift flour and salt together. Mix with egg and milk, beat well. Leave to stand for 30 minutes before using. Cook as above.

Borscht with yogurt (*top*, see page 49), Chestnut soup (*center*, see page 50), Tomato and zucchini soup (*bottom*, see page 52)

BEVERAGES

Milk shake See photograph, page 41 ✷ W M E

Serves 4

420 ml/1¾ cups milk substitute   *1 banana*
420 ml/1¾ cups fruit juice

Blend together in an electric blender, or mash banana and whip with milk and fruit juice. Chill before serving.

Variations   This is very refreshing made with pineapple juice.
  Fruits such as strawberries and apricots could be substituted for the fruit juice and banana in the recipe.

Carob milk drink   ✷ W M E

Serves 2

1 tsp honey   *300 ml/1¼ cups milk substitute*
15 g/1 tbsp carob flour

Whip together or blend in an electric blender. Chill, or serve hot.

Minty yogurt   ✷ W M E

Serves 2

300 ml/1¼ cups goat's or ewe's yogurt 1 tbsp fresh chopped mint

Whip or blend together in an electric blender the yogurt, mint and up to 120 ml/½ cup water, depending on thickness of the yogurt. Chill.
  Very good served with Indian food.

Pineapple yogurt drink   ✷ W M E

Serves 2

240 ml/1 cup goat's or ewe's yogurt   2 tsp sugar (optional)
180 ml/¾ cup pineapple juice

Whip together or blend in an electric blender. Chill before serving.

Fruit cocktail

Serves 4   See photograph, page 43

600 ml/2½ cups apple juice
60 g/4 tbsp chopped fruit, eg, peach,
banana, cucumber

Mix together and chill before serving.

Spiced apple juice

Serves 4

420 ml/1¾ cups apple juice   *⅛ tsp ginger*
180 ml/¾ cup water   *⅛ tsp nutmeg*
6 cloves   *2 tsp honey (optional)*
⅛ tsp cinnamon

Put all ingredients into a saucepan. Heat but do not boil. Allow
the spices to infuse for a few minutes. Strain before serving.
  Makes a warming winter drink.

Coconut milk

Makes 600 ml/2½ cups

85 g/1 cup flaked coconut   *15 ml/1 tbsp honey*
300 ml/1¼ cups water

Add coconut to water and bring to simmering point slowly.
Remove from heat, cool and purée in an electric blender until
smooth. Strain through a fine sieve, pressing out as much of the
liquid as possible. Return coconut to saucepan and repeat using
the same quantity of water; simmer, liquidize and sieve. Mix both
batches of milk with the honey. Chill and store in the refrigerator.
Stir before serving.
  Can be used as a drink or in desserts or on cereals.

APPETIZERS AND SOUPS

Cocktail nibbles

1 avocado
salt and pepper

Garnishes:
tomato, sliced
cucumber, sliced

fresh boiled beets, cubed
chopped chives or parsley
stuffed olives

puffed rice cakes (available from
  health food shops)

Cut the avocado in half, remove the pit and scoop out the flesh. Mash the flesh and season to taste. Halve or quarter the rice cakes with a sharp knife and spread with the mashed avocado. Decorate with any of the suggested garnishes. (See photograph, page 43.)

Variation Feta cheese can also be served sliced on rice cakes and decorated.

Melon and grape savory appetizer

Serves 2–3   See photograph, page 42

half a 450 g/1 lb honeydew melon,
  chilled
60 g/⅓ cup black grapes, chilled
1½ tsp apple juice

3 tsp sunflower oil
salt and pepper
chopped chives

Scrape the seeds out of the melon, and either scoop out balls with a special cutter, or cube the flesh. Halve the grapes, removing seeds if necessary. Mix the apple juice, oil, seasoning and chives. Pour over the fruit, toss and serve immediately (otherwise the dark grapes may discolor the melon).

Avocado provençal

Serves 2

20 g/2 tbsp green pepper, chopped
20 g/2 tbsp cucumber, chopped
1 tsp tomato paste
3 tsp apple juice
½ small clove garlic, finely sliced or
  crushed through press

1 avocado
salt and pepper
⅛ tsp cayenne pepper
1 tbsp chopped parsley to garnish

Place the green pepper and cucumber in a small bowl. Make a dressing of the tomato paste, apple juice, garlic and seasoning. Pour over the vegetables and stir together well. Cover with plastic wrap and leave in the refrigerator for 30 minutes to allow the flavors to blend (but not so long that the vegetables lose their crunchiness).

Cut the avocado in two, remove pit, fill the hollows with mixture, and serve garnished with fresh parsley.

Spinach roulade See photograph, page 42

Serves 6 as an appetizer

280 g/1 10-oz package frozen chopped spinach, defrosted
30 g/2 tbsp Kosher margarine
salt and pepper

½ tsp grated nutmeg
4 medium-size eggs
2 ripe avocados
1–2 tsp apple juice

Preheat oven to 350 °F/180 °C.

Line a 30 cm/12 in jelly roll pan with waxed paper rubbed with a little Kosher margarine.

Heat the spinach in a pan with the margarine, salt and pepper to taste, and nutmeg.

Separate the eggs: beat the whites until they hold peaks and the yolks until creamy.

Beat the spinach mixture into the yolks, then fold in the whites. Pour into the prepared pan and spread evenly with a spatula.

Bake for 20 minutes or until the top is just firm.

Cool in the pan to room temperature then cool further in the refrigerator for 30–60 minutes. Cover with a damp cloth and leave at room temperature for an additional 30 minutes. Invert pan on to a board so that the roulade comes out with the cloth underneath. Peel off the waxed paper.

Scoop out the avocado flesh and mash with salt and pepper and as much apple juice as required to give a consistency that will spread easily.

Spread it on the baked mixture and carefully roll it up by holding up the edges of the cloth.

Borscht See photograph, page 44

Serves 3

450 g/1 lb raw beets
2 stalks celery, chopped
900 ml/3¾ cups meat stock (see page 79)

salt and pepper
chopped chives and goat's or sheep's yogurt to garnish

Peel and coarsely grate the beets into a pan. Add the celery, stock and seasoning. Bring to a boil and simmer uncovered for 45 minutes. Strain and adjust seasoning. Serve in bowls, garnished with yogurt and chives.

Note: To avoid staining your hands wear rubber gloves when peeling and grating the beets.

Celeriac soup

[*] [W] [M] [E]

Serves 2

1 celeriac, pared and cubed
300 ml/1¼ cups milk substitute
120 ml/½ cup water
salt and pepper
parsley to garnish

Put celeriac in a pan with milk substitute and water. Bring to a boil and simmer for 10–15 minutes, or until cooked. Purée in an electric blender and strain the mixture. Adjust seasoning – extra salt takes away any bitterness – and reheat.

Serve garnished with a sprig of parsley.

Chestnut soup

[*] [W] [M] [E]

Serves 4

See photograph, page 44

170 g/1 cup dried chestnuts, soaked for 24 hours (see below)
2 onions, roughly chopped
2 carrots, diced
2 stalks celery, diced
⅛ tsp thyme
½ tsp grated nutmeg
salt and pepper
150–300 ml/⅝–1¼ cups milk substitute
parsley to garnish

Place chestnuts in a bowl. Pour in 1.2 liters/5 cups boiling water and leave to soak for at least 24 hours. Place chestnuts and liquid in a saucepan and add onions, carrots and celery. Simmer for about 1½ hours or until chestnuts are soft; or cook for ½ hour in pressure cooker. Purée in an electric blender, return to saucepan, add herbs and salt and pepper to taste, and thin with milk substitute.

Reheat to serve, but do not boil. Garnish with parsley before serving.

Chicken and mushroom soup

Serves 2

[*] [W] [M] [E]

1 chicken carcass
300 ml/1¼ cups water
salt and pepper
100 g/1½ cups chopped mushrooms
30 g/2 tbsp lentils
300 ml/1¼ cups vegetable stock (see page 79)
60 ml/¼ cup milk substitute

Boil the chicken carcass in the water with seasonings for 1–1½ hours or 15–20 minutes in a pressure cooker at high pressure.

Remove bones and skin from the stock.

Add the mushrooms, lentils and vegetable stock. Cook for an additional 20 minutes or 5 minutes in a pressure cooker. Adjust seasoning. Stir in milk substitute and serve immediately.

Gazpacho   ✹ W M E

Serves 3

1 medium cucumber, chopped
225 g/½ lb ripe tomatoes, skinned
  and chopped
60 g/6 tbsp green or red pepper,
  chopped
1 clove garlic, crushed

15 ml/1 tbsp sunflower oil
15 ml/1 tbsp tomato paste
salt and pepper
chives to garnish
240 ml/1 cup water

Mix all the ingredients in a bowl and purée in an electric blender.

Transfer to a serving dish and chill, covered with plastic wrap for 1–2 hours.

If too thick, dilute with a little ice water or a couple of ice cubes. Serve garnished with chopped chives.

Leek soup   ✹ W M E

Serves 3–4

2 medium-sized leeks, chopped
4 small carrots, chopped
300 ml/1¼ cups salted water
150 ml/⅝ cup milk substitute

salt and pepper
30 g/2 tbsp chopped cooked chicken
  (optional)

Cook the vegetables in salted water for 10–15 minutes or until tender. Purée in an electric blender, and return to the pan, adding the milk substitute and adjusting the seasoning. Add the chicken if used. Bring to a boil, simmer and cook for 2 or 3 minutes. Serve.

Quick snack lunch soup   ✹ W M E

Serves 1

50 g/⅓ cup chopped carrot
50 g/⅓ cup chopped celery
20 g/1½ tbsp lentils
salt and pepper to taste

2 tsp tomato paste
300 ml/1¼ cups water
parsley to garnish

Simmer all the ingredients together for 20 minutes or until soft. Purée in an electric blender. Reheat. Serve garnished with parsley.

Tomato and zucchini soup [*] [W] [M] [E]

Serves 4 See photograph, page 44

225 g/½ lb zucchini, trimmed
225 g/½ lb ripe tomatoes, skinned
1 liter/4½ cups milk substitute
1 tbsp chopped parsley
sprig thyme
salt and pepper

Steam the zucchini until tender. Chop and mix with tomatoes, milk substitute, parsley, thyme leaves, salt and pepper to taste. Purée in an electric blender. Place in a pan, bring to a boil, adjust seasoning and serve.

Variation This can also be served as an iced summer soup: chill the mixture and, if you like, add ice cubes before serving.

SALADS AND VEGETABLES

Apple and bean salad [*] [W] [M] [E]

Serves 4

450 g/1 lb frozen lima beans, cooked and allowed to cool
1 Granny Smith apple, cored and chopped
30 ml/2 tbsp olive oil
30 ml/2 tbsp apple juice
1½ tsp chopped parsley
1½ tsp chopped chives
salt and freshly ground black pepper

Mix the beans and apple in a big bowl. Add the olive oil, apple juice, herbs and seasoning and stir well.

Cover and leave to marinate in the refrigerator for 2–3 hours, stirring occasionally, before serving.

This is a convenient and appetizing addition to a lunch box.

The devil's own drumsticks (*top*, see page 65), Apple and bean salad (*bottom*)

Chickpea salad

Serves 2–4

*250 g/1¼ cups chickpeas, soaked
overnight in water*
30 ml/2 tbsp olive oil

2 cloves garlic, crushed
salt and pepper
1 tbsp chopped parsley to garnish

Drain the chickpeas, place in a large saucepan, cover with water, bring to a boil and simmer for 3–3½ hours, or cook in a pressure cooker for 15 minutes at high pressure.
   Stir in the oil, garlic and seasoning. Serve hot or cold, garnished with parsley.

Variation   Skinned and sliced tomatoes can also be added to the salad.

Chicken Waldorf

Serves 2

*150–200 g/1–1½ cups cold cooked
chicken, chopped*
2 stalks celery, chopped
1 eating apple, cored and chopped

60 g/½ cup chopped walnuts
salt and freshly ground black pepper
75 ml/⅓ cup goat's yogurt
watercress to garnish

Combine the chicken, celery, apple and nuts in a serving bowl. Season, add the yogurt and toss. Garnish with watercress.

Feta salad

Serves 4

225 g/½ lb feta cheese
1 crisp lettuce
60 g/½ cup black olives
225 g/½ lb tomatoes

Dressing:
30 ml/2 tbsp olive oil
2 cloves garlic, crushed
salt and pepper

The cheese can be crumbled into the salad or served separately.
   Finely chop the lettuce and mix with olives and sliced tomatoes. Mix oil, garlic and seasoning and pour over salad. Toss and serve.

Note: Add lemon juice to the dressing if allowed.

Feta salad (*top*), Brown rice and lentils (*center right*, see page 61), Pakoras (*center left*, see page 59), Raita (*bottom*, see page 86)

Curried rice salad

W   M   E

Serves 4–6

225 g/1¼ cups brown rice

¼ tsp cayenne pepper (optional)

Dressing:
30 ml/2 tbsp sunflower oil
7 ml/½ tbsp apple juice
curry powder (make sure it is wheat-
   free) to taste (about 3 tsp)*

170 g/1½ cups chopped apple
60 g/½ cup chopped walnuts
60 g/⅓ cup golden or seedless raisins
120 g/½ cup chopped red or green
   pepper

Cook the rice (see page 25). Drain. Stir the dressing ingredients together in a bowl. Pour over the rice while still warm and mix well. Add the other salad ingredients when the rice is cool and toss lightly.

Variations   Add celery, cucumber, bananas.

Sweet salad

★   W   M   E

Serves 2

60 g/½ cup kohlrabi or rutabaga
100 g/1 cup small cauliflower florets
1 handful golden raisins

salt and freshly ground black pepper
30 g/2 tbsp sheep's yogurt cheese
sliced mushrooms to garnish

Coarsely grate the kohlrabi and mix with the cauliflower. Add the golden raisins and seasoning.
    In a separate bowl mix the cheese with 60 ml/¼ cup water to produce a thin paste. Pour over the vegetable mixture and stir well. Chill for 1 hour. Stir again and garnish with the mushrooms, just before serving.
    This is a handy and filling snack to put in a lunch box.

Chinese-style cabbage

Serves 4

15 ml/1 tbsp sunflower oil
1 clove garlic, crushed
½ large white cabbage, shredded
1 tsp light brown sugar
salt and pepper

⅛ tsp paprika
100 g/⅞ cup chopped almonds
15 g/1 tbsp ginger root, peeled and
   finely chopped

Heat the oil in a saucepan and fry the garlic until golden. Add the cabbage, sugar, salt, pepper, paprika and 4 tbsp water. Simmer

*If you prefer, the curry powder can be cooked before adding: heat 2 tsp oil and fry 1 crushed clove garlic and 3 tsp curry powder very gently for 2 minutes. Turn this into the rice with all the other ingredients.

gently, removing lid to stir occasionally for 5–10 minutes, until the cabbage is nearly cooked. Add almonds and ginger and cook for another couple of minutes.
Serve hot.

Glazed carrots

Serves 2

60 g/4 tbsp Kosher margarine
450 g/1 lb young carrots scraped and
  left whole
3 tsp sugar

30 g/2 tbsp brown rice miso dissolved
  in 300 ml/1¼ cups hot, not boiling
  water
freshly ground pepper
chopped parsley to garnish

Melt margarine in a saucepan. Add carrots, sugar, salt and enough miso mixture to come halfway up the carrots. Cook gently without a lid, stirring occasionally until soft. Remove carrots and keep hot.
  Boil liquid rapidly until reduced to a rich glaze. Roll the carrots in it until they are well coated. Season with pepper and garnish with parsley.

Chinese-style cauliflower and pole beans

Serves 2

225 g/½ lb pole beans (fresh or
  frozen), strings removed and sliced
¼ average-sized cauliflower (fresh or
  frozen), broken into florets
60 ml/4 tbsp sunflower oil

12 blanched almonds
1 clove garlic, crushed
1 tsp sugar
1 tsp paprika
salt and pepper

Cook vegetables in salted water for 5 minutes and drain.
  Heat oil in a large skillet and fry the almonds and garlic for 1 minute or until golden.
  Add beans and cauliflower, sugar, paprika and seasoning to taste. Fry, stirring over a low heat for 2–3 minutes.

Parsnip chips

Serves 2

450 g/1 lb parsnips
sunflower oil as required

salt and pepper

Pare the parsnips and cut into circles about 5 mm/¼ in thick. Cover the bottom of a heavy-based skillet with oil. Heat the oil and when it is medium-hot, slip in the parsnip slices and let them sizzle briefly. Turn down heat and let them cook through, then turn up heat and brown them (the whole process should take less than 5 minutes).

Drain on paper towels, season to taste and serve immediately.

Creamed spinach

Serves 2

675 g/1½ lb spinach
60 g/4 tbsp Kosher margarine

60 ml/¼ cup milk substitute
½ tsp ground nutmeg

Wash and drain the spinach well. Cook in a large pan with the Kosher margarine for 10 minutes or until the spinach is soft and the fluid reduced. Add nutmeg and milk substitute, and continue cooking until the spinach is almost dry but still creamy.

Baked sweet potatoes

Serves 4–6

450 g/1 lb sweet potatoes, peeled
*   and diced*
150 ml/⅝ cup milk substitute
2 eggs
60 ml/¼ cup oil (sunflower,
*   safflower, soy)*

⅛ tsp salt
¼ tsp ground ginger
¼ tsp ground cinnamon
15 g/1 tbsp brown rice miso, mixed to a
*   paste with a little water*
60 ml/4 tbsp honey

Preheat the oven to 350 °F/180 °C.

Purée all the ingredients together briefly in an electric blender so that you have a coarse mixture. Place in a greased casserole dish and bake for 45 minutes.

This is a sweet vegetable which goes very well with pork or chicken dishes.

Variation   Yams can be used instead of sweet potatoes.

VEGETARIAN DISHES

Pakoras See photograph, page 54   ✶   W   M   E

Serves 4

Batter:
225 g/1½ cups chickpea flour
½ tsp commercial wheat-free baking
  powder (see page 89)
1 tsp salt
½ tsp ground coriander
1 tsp garam masala
½ tsp chili powder
½ tsp ground cumin

Vegetables – use one or a combination of the following:
diced stalks and florets of cauliflower
diced eggplant
onion rings

oil for frying (soy, sunflower,
  safflower)

Sieve all the dry ingredients into a bowl. Add sufficient water
(about 300 ml/1¼ cups) to make a thick batter and beat well. Add
the vegetables to the batter mixture.

Deep fry the pakoras: drop 1 tbsp of batter mixture at a time
into the medium-hot oil (do not overcrowd the pan) and cook
until golden brown.

Drain and serve immediately with salad and raita (see page
86).

Note: For those who like spicy food, the quantity of spices can be
increased in the batter mixture.

Vegetables au gratin   ✶   W   M   E

Serves 4

1 cauliflower broken into florets (fresh
  or 450 g/1 lb frozen)
3 large carrots, pared and cut into
  circles
120 g/6 brussels sprouts (fresh or
  frozen)

salt
120 g/generous 1 cup bean sprouts
200 g/¾ cup feta cheese, cut up
sliced tomato and chopped parsley to
  garnish

Cook all the vegetables except the bean sprouts in boiling salted
water until just firm to bite. Drain and put into a shallow flameproof dish with the bean sprouts. Sprinkle with cheese.

Place under the broiler until the cheese is browned.

Serve garnished with tomato and parsley.

Mediterranean vegetables ✷ Ⓦ Ⓜ Ⓔ

Serves 2

340 g/2 zucchini, finely sliced
200 g/½ large eggplant, finely sliced
salt and pepper
30–60 g/2–4 tbsp Kosher margarine

340 g/1½ cups tomatoes, skinned
and sliced
dried thyme and basil
60 g/¼ cup feta cheese
30 ml/2 tbsp olive oil

Preheat oven to 400 °F/200 °C.
Season zucchini and eggplant and sauté separately in the margarine. Season tomatoes.
Grease a small casserole with Kosher margarine and layer the vegetables – at least 2 layers of each – ending with a layer of zucchini. Sprinkle with a pinch of thyme and basil. Crumble the feta cheese on top and pour the olive oil over the mixture.
Bake for 15–20 minutes.

Stuffed tomatoes ✷ Ⓦ Ⓜ Ⓔ

Serves 2–4

675 g/1½ lb tomatoes – 4 large
tomatoes or 2 large beefsteak
salt and pepper
120 g/⅜ cup brown rice
1 stalk celery, grated
1 medium-sized green pepper, cored
and finely chopped

2 cloves garlic, crushed
15 g/1 tbsp Kosher margarine
handful of parsley, chopped
1 tbsp chopped mint
15 g/1 tbsp currants, chopped
30 ml/2 tbsp olive oil

Cut the tops off the tomatoes and set them aside. Scoop out the pulp and set aside (take care not to remove too much flesh or the tomatoes will split when cooked). Sprinkle the tomato shells lightly with salt, invert them and let them drain.
Preheat oven to 350 °F/180 °C.
Partially cook rice in boiling water until it begins to soften. Drain.
Fry the celery, pepper, and garlic gently in Kosher margarine until almost done. Chop the tomato pulp and add it to the fried vegetables with the herbs, seasonings and currants. Simmer for 3 minutes and remove from the heat. Add rice to this mixture, strain off most of the excess juice and reserve.
Stuff the tomatoes with the rice and vegetable mixture and replace the reserved tops. Arrange in shallow baking dish. Add the olive oil to the reserved juice to make a gravy and pour it around the stuffed tomatoes.
Bake for 40 minutes in the oven, basting occasionally to prevent the outsides from drying out.
Serve hot or cold as a snack meal or accompaniment to another dish.

Brown rice and lentils

Serves 2–4 See photograph, page 54

225 g/1¼ cups brown rice
170 g/⅞ cup lentils
2 stalks celery, chopped
1 clove garlic, crushed
1 handful parsley, chopped

15 ml/1 tbsp oil (sunflower, safflower, soy)
½ tsp sea salt
½ tsp ground cumin
30 g/2 tbsp brown rice miso, mixed to a paste with a little water

Cook rice (see page 25). Drain.
 Wash lentils and cook for 15 minutes in 900 ml/3¾ cups water. Sauté celery, garlic and parsley in oil. Add rice and vegetables to the lentils and simmer until thick. Add salt, cumin, and miso to taste.
 Serve hot with a salad.

Variations Any allowed vegetables can be added.
 Leftovers can be shaped into patties and fried in oil.

Buckwheat croquettes

Serves 2

170 g/1 cup buckwheat groats
2 stalks celery, grated
30 g/¼ cup soybean flour

salt and pepper
herbs as desired, eg, parsley, sage
30 ml/2 tbsp oil

Cook buckwheat groats (see page 25). Drain and cool. Add celery, soybean flour, seasonings and herbs, and stir until evenly mixed. Shape into 1-cm/½ in-thick patties. Fry in oil, on both sides, until cooked.
 Serve with apple sauce or tomato sauce (see page 85), or tahini gravy (see page 80).

Kidney bean lasagne

Serves 4–6

225 g/1¼ cups kidney beans, soaked in water overnight
1 large onion, chopped
15 ml/1 tbsp oil
450 g/1 lb tomatoes, skinned and chopped
2 stalks celery, grated
4 whole cloves

1 tbsp chopped fresh majoram or 1 tsp dried
2 cloves garlic, crushed
salt and pepper
½ recipe buckwheat pasta (see page 63)
120 g/½ cup feta cheese, crumbled

Drain the beans. Place in a large pan with plenty of fresh water and boil for 1–1½ hours or cook in a pressure cooker for 15 minutes at high pressure. Drain.

Fry the onion in the oil until soft. Add all the other ingredients, except the beans cheese, and pasta. Simmer in a covered pan for 10 minutes. Mix in the beans.

Preheat oven to 350 °F/180 °C.

Make the pasta, roll out and cut into rectangular sheets.

Cook the pasta in boiling water for 2–3 minutes. Remove each sheet individually from the pan and drain (if drained together in a colander they will stick together). Grease a shallow dish and arrange in it layers of bean mixture, cheese and pasta, ending with beans and cheese. Bake for 30 minutes.

Variations   1. For a moister dish, make a sauce using milk substitute thickened with rice flour and layer this with the bean mixture and cheese.

2. Make a filling of cooked spinach with feta cheese, and top with a white sauce and grated cheese.

Stuffed eggplant $\boxed{W}$ $\boxed{M}$ $\boxed{E}$

Serves 2

2 large eggplants
sesame seeds
olive oil
450 g/1 lb tomatoes, skinned and
* chopped*
3 cloves garlic, crushed

1 small onion, chopped
30 g/¼ cup millet flakes
½ tsp dried basil
salt and pepper
60 g/¼ cup feta cheese

Preheat oven to 400 °F/200 °C.

Cut eggplants lengthwise, lay in an ovenproof dish, and sprinkle with sesame seeds and a little oil. Bake for about 20 minutes, or until soft. Cool a little and scoop out pulp. Reserve the shells.

Simmer tomatoes, garlic, onion, millet, herbs and seasoning for 10 minutes. Mix with eggplant flesh.

Fill the shells with this mixture and top with crumbled feta cheese. Bake for 30 minutes until it is heated through and the cheese has melted.

Serve with salad.

Ratatouille $\boxed{\bigstar}$ $\boxed{W}$ $\boxed{M}$ $\boxed{E}$

Serves 4

3 cloves garlic, crushed
1 large or 2 small eggplants, sliced
1 large green pepper, sliced
60 g/½ cup sliced cucmber
225 g/1½ cups sliced zucchini

450 g/1 lb tomatoes, skinned
1 tsp honey
salt and freshly ground black pepper
75 ml/5 tbsp olive oil

Season the vegetables generously with black pepper and lightly with salt. Add the honey and simmer them gently in the oil in a pan with a closely fitting lid for approximately 1 hour, stirring occasionally.

Buckwheat pasta · Ⓦ Ⓜ

Serves 4

225 g/2¼ cups buckwheat flour   *1 small egg*
22 g/1½ tbsp Kosher margarine   *salt*

Sift the flour into a bowl and make a well in the center. Put in the margarine, egg and a pinch of salt. Mix thoroughly, adding a little water to make a thick dough. Knead well until the dough is smooth. If the mixture is too sticky, add more flour.

Roll out the dough on a lightly floured surface, using buckwheat or rice flour, until the pasta is very thin. Cut into required shapes.

Place the pasta into a large pan containing plenty of salted boiling water. A little oil can be added to the water to prevent the pasta from sticking together. Boil uncovered for 3–5 minutes, until just tender but firm to bite. Do not overcook.

Drain in a colander and serve immediately.

Good served with a sauce, such as meat sauce, cheese or tomato, or lasagne (see page 61).

Variation If you find the taste of buckwheat too strong, use half rice flour and half buckwheat.

SNACKS

Baked beans · ✴ Ⓦ Ⓜ Ⓔ

Serves 2–4

225 g/1 cup navy beans, soaked over-   *300 ml/1¼ cups basic tomato sauce*
  night in cold water   *(see page 85)*
                                     salt and pepper

Drain the beans and place in a large pan with plenty of water. Boil for 1–1½ hours or cook in pressure cooker for 6 minutes at high pressure. Drain. Mix with the tomato sauce, adjust seasoning and heat through.

Can be served hot or cold.

Note: Chili powder can be added to the sauce if liked.

Lima bean brunch

Serves 2

*100 g/⅔ cup lima beans, soaked in
  cold water overnight*
30 ml/2 tbsp sunflower oil
*225 g/½ lb tomatoes, coarsely
  chopped*

*100 g/⅔ cup green pepper, seeded
  and chopped*
*30 g/2 tbsp brown rice miso, mixed to a
  paste with a little water*
60 g/1 cup chopped mushrooms
salt and pepper

Drain the beans and place in a large pan with plenty of water. Boil for 1–1½ hours or cook in a pressure cooker for 10 minutes at high pressure. Drain.

Heat the oil in a pan and fry the tomatoes and peppers gently for 10 minutes. Add the beans, miso mixture, mushrooms and seasoning and simmer for another 10 minutes.

Italian tomatoes

Sufficient to cover 4 slices bread

340 g/¾ lb tomatoes
3 cloves garlic, crushed

7 ml/½ tbsp olive oil
chopped fresh basil to garnish

Pour boiling water over the tomatoes, then drain after 1 minute. Plunge into cold water, drain and peel. Chop the tomatoes, add the garlic and oil, and cook on low heat for 10 minutes.

Serve on wheat-free toast sprinkled with chopped basil.

Pizza

Serves 2

280 g/2¼ cups rice flour
½ tsp salt
7 g/1 package active dry yeast
1 egg
olive oil

Filling:
*tomato sauce (see page 85), anchovies,
  black olives, peppers, feta cheese,
  dried oregano*

Place the flour and salt in a mixing bowl. Crumble in the yeast. Beat the egg and add it to the flour with enough lukewarm water to make a stiff dough. Knead dough lightly. Divide in half and press into 2 round greased pans, 23 cm/9 in in diameter. Brush the tops with olive oil.

Layer the filling generously over the pizza base and sprinkle with oregano.

Preheat oven to 450 °F/230 °C.

Allow pizzas to rise. Bake for 10 minutes, then turn oven down to 400 °F/200 °C, and cook for an additional 25 minutes.

Serve with a salad.

The devil's own drumsticks

See photograph, page 53

As many chicken drumsticks as   *cayenne pepper to taste*
   required (thaw thoroughly if frozen)   *salt and pepper*
chickpea flour for coating

Coat the drumsticks in chickpea flour seasoned with salt, pepper and cayenne. Broil for 20–30 minutes, turning frequently.

Serve hot or cold.

These are especially good to take on picnics or to work for lunch.

FISH

Quick cod in mushroom sauce

Serves 2

2 frozen cod steaks, defrosted   *15 g/2 tbsp soy flour*
30 g/2 tbsp Kosher margarine   *120 ml/½ cup milk substitute*
   100 g/1 cup button mushrooms, sliced
Sauce: *salt and pepper*
15 g/1 tbsp Kosher margarine   *parsley to garnish*

Dot the cod with margarine and broil for about 6 minutes on each side.

To make sauce, melt the margarine and make a roux by adding the flour, then gradually stir in the milk substitute. Add the mushrooms and season to taste. Simmer and stir for a couple of minutes.

Place the cod steaks on a warmed serving dish and pour the sauce over them. Garnish with fresh parsley if available.

Flaked fish with vegetable rice

Serves 2

170 g/1 cup brown rice	*1 handful parsley, chopped*
225 g/½ lb white fish	*30 g/2 tbsp Kosher margarine*
170 g/1 cup cooked vegetables (eg,	*cayenne pepper*
peas, diced carrots, chopped celery)	*sea salt*

Cook the rice (see page 25) and drain.

Poach the fish in water for 10 minutes. Discard skin and bones and flake fish. Combine the fish, rice, vegetables and parsley and toss in the margarine. Add seasoning to taste.

Serve hot.

Crispy coated fish

Serves 2

175 g/¾ cup millet	*milk substitute*
2 haddock fillets, about 280 g/10 oz	*salt and pepper*

Lightly grind the millet in a coffee grinder until it resembles bread crumbs. Moisten the fillets with milk substitute, then roll them in the millet. Fry in oil.

Variation   Any other fish fillet, such as cod or flounder can be used.

Stuffed mackerel

Serves 2

2 medium-sized apples, pared, cored	*30 g/2 tbsp lightly ground millet*
and sliced	*2 mackerel, boned*
85 g/¾ cup celery, washed and	*150 ml/⅜ cup apple juice*
chopped	*1 level tsp arrowroot*
1–2 tsp sunflower oil	*1 level tsp sugar*
salt and pepper	

Preheat oven to 350 °F/180 °C.

Fry apples and celery in oil until the apples are soft. Season and stir in the millet.

Spread this stuffing inside each fish and place in an ovenproof dish with a little of the apple juice.

Bake in the oven for 25–30 minutes. When almost done, mix the arrowroot and sugar with a little of the apple juice. Heat the remainder of the apple juice and stir into the paste, then return it all to the heat, until it thickens and clears.

Pour a little of the glaze over the fish; serve the rest separately as a sauce.

Mackerel with gooseberries ✦ W M E

Serves 2

2 mackerel fillets
60 g/4 tbsp lightly ground millet
salt and pepper
knob of Kosher margarine

100 g/¾ cup gooseberries – fresh
1 tsp sugar
⅛ tsp grated nutmeg

Wash and dry mackerel fillets. Season ground millet and sprinkle over mackerel. Dot with the margarine and cook under a preheated broiler 15–20 minutes.

Stew the gooseberries with 1 tbsp water, sugar and nutmeg. Rub through a sieve to remove the seeds.

Place mackerel on a warmed serving dish and pour on the gooseberry sauce. Serve immediately.

This dish is good served with zucchini and fresh small carrots.

Simple trout ✦ W M E

Serves 1

See photograph, page 71

15 g/1 tbsp Kosher margarine
1–2 tbsp chopped parsley

salt and pepper
1 trout, gutted and cleaned

Mix the margarine, parsley and seasoning into a soft ball. Place most of the mixture inside the fish and dot the remainder on the outside. Broil under a moderate heat, 5–10 minutes on each side.

Serve with fresh green vegetables.

Baked salmon ✦ W M E

Serves 6

900 g/2 lb piece of salmon
Kosher margarine

salt and pepper
chopped parsley

Preheat oven to 300 °F/150 °C.

Wipe the fish, removing the fins and any blood near the backbone. Grease a large piece of aluminum foil with margarine. Place the fish in the center, season it lightly with salt and pepper and scatter the parsley over it. Wrap it loosely in the foil, and place on a baking sheet. Bake for 1¼–1¾ hours, depending on the thickness of the fish, but be careful not to overcook.

Serve hot. If you want to serve it cold, remove the skin while the fish is still warm.

Serve with a salad.

MEAT

Chili con carne

Serves 2

150 g/¾ cup dried red kidney beans, soaked overnight in cold water
225 g/½ lb ground beef
½ average-sized green pepper, coarsely chopped
4 tomatoes
1 green chili pepper, seeded and chopped
30 ml/2 tbsp tomato paste
salt and pepper

Heat a heavy-bottomed casserole or pan and brown the meat. Drain and add the beans, green pepper, tomatoes and chili. Stir in the tomato paste and enough water to cover, bring to a boil, boil for 10 minutes, then turn down heat and and simmer for 1½ hours or until the beans are cooked.

Alternatively, cook the beans separately in advance (1–1½ hours in boiling water, or 10 minutes in a pressure cooker at high pressure), then add to the cooked chili and reheat.

Risotto with beef

Serves 2

60 g/4 tbsp Kosher margarine
2 stalks celery, cleaned and chopped
225 g/½ lb ground beef
225 g/1¼ cups brown rice, washed
⅛ tsp nutmeg
sea salt and pepper
1 tsp dried basil
120 g/½ cup chopped tomatoes
30 g/2 tbsp brown rice miso mixed to a thick paste with a little water

Heat the margarine in a saucepan. Sauté the celery and ground beef. When the beef has browned, add the rice and heat gently for about 10 minutes. Stir occasionally.

Sprinkle in the nutmeg, salt and pepper and basil. Cover with water and add the tomatoes. Cook gently for 45 minutes, adding more water if necessary to prevent the mixture drying out. When the rice is cooked and the water absorbed, stir in the miso.

Serve hot with salad.

Liver with thyme and garlic

Serves 4

sunflower oil as needed
1 clove garlic, thinly sliced
450 g/1 lb lamb's liver, thinly sliced
1½ tsp dried thyme
salt and pepper
15 ml/1 tbsp apple juice

Heat the oil and fry the garlic in it for a couple of minutes. Add the liver and brown quickly on both sides. Add the thyme, salt, pepper and apple juice and mix well. Cook for another minute, and serve immediately.

and apple juice and mix well. Cook for another minute, and serve immediately.

Bombay burgers ⊠ W M E

Serves 2

225 g/½ lb ground beef
¼ medium-sized green pepper, finely chopped
1 clove garlic, crushed
1½ tsp tomato paste
15 g/1 tbsp chickpea flour

⅛ tsp each of: ground cumin, chili powder, coriander, cinnamon, ginger, nutmeg and cloves
salt and pepper
30 ml/2 tbsp apple juice

Place the meat, green pepper, garlic, tomato paste, half the flour, spices, salt and pepper in a bowl and mix well, adding enough apple juice to give the mixture a firm consistency. Shape into burgers and dust with the remaining flour.

Cook under a preheated broiler for 10–15 minutes, turning occasionally until browned.

Serve with rice and a salad.

Four-meat pâté ⊠ W M E

12 generous portions

675 g/1½ lb lamb's liver
225 g/½ lb chicken liver
225 g/½ lb lean veal
450 g/1 lb lean pork
100 g/½ cup chopped green pepper
100 g/1½ cups sliced mushrooms

2 cloves garlic
2 level tsp salt
2 level tsp fresh ground black pepper
2 level tsp dried basil
1–2 tomatoes, sliced

Preheat the oven to 350 °F/180 °C.

Grind together all the meats, the green pepper, mushrooms and garlic. Mix well, adding the salt, pepper and basil. Spoon the mixture into an ovenproof dish or dishes and top with slices of tomato. Cover with foil and place in a larger pan containing sufficient hot water to come halfway up the side of the dish. Bake for 2½–3 hours. When cool, cover with fresh foil, weigh down and leave in a cool place.

Served with buckwheat pancakes, savory rice cakes and salad, or savory buckwheat crackers, this pâté is particularly useful for snacks and packed lunches.

Rosemary and garlic lamb ⊠ W M E

Serves 2

30 g/1 tbsp chopped green pepper
1 large clove garlic, crushed
30 ml/2 tbsp sunflower oil

170–200 g/1¼–1½ cups cold cooked lamb, coarsely chopped
3 tsp millet flour

30 g/2 tbsp brown rice miso mixed to a
   thick paste with a little water
¼ tsp dried rosemary

salt and pepper
parsley to garnish

Fry the green pepper and garlic in the oil until soft. Add the meat, and fry an additional 5 minutes. Stir in the flour, the miso and the rosemary and season to taste.

Simmer for 10–15 minutes then serve on brown rice, garnished with parsley.

Balkan chops

Serves 2

60 ml/4 tbsp apple juice
15 ml/1 tbsp sunflower oil
salt and pepper
⅛ tsp dried thyme
2 lamb chops

½ clove garlic, finely sliced
75 g/⅓ cup plain goat's or ewe's
   yogurt
1 tsp paprika

Preheat oven to 375 °F/190 °C.

Mix together the apple juice, oil, seasoning and thyme. Marinate the chops in this mixture for 2–3 hours. Drain the chops and place in a shallow ovenproof dish with the sliced garlic. Cover with foil and bake for 45–60 minutes or until cooked through.

Pour any gravy from around the chops into a bowl, skim off fat and keep hot.

Mix the yogurt and paprika and spoon over the chops. Return to the oven for 15 minutes, this time uncovered.

Garnish with a little paprika and serve the gravy separately.

Meaty zucchini

Serves 4

225 g/½ lb ground beef
1 small eggplant, sliced
⅓ medium-sized green pepper, chopped
4 tomatoes, chopped
120 g/¼ lb large button mushrooms,
   sliced

oregano and basil
salt and pepper
2 tsp tomato paste
2 large zucchini
15 g/1 tbsp brown rice miso dissolved
   in 150 ml/⅝ cup hot water

Heat a skillet and fry the beef until browned. Move the meat to the side of the pan and fry the eggplant, green pepper, tomatoes and mushrooms in the beef fat. Add the herbs and seasoning, and stir in the tomato paste.

Simple trout (*top*, see page 67), Balkan chops (*bottom*)

Cut the zucchini into thick slices. Pare, scoop out the centers, and arrange on the base of a large shallow casserole. Spoon the meat mixture into the middle of the zucchini rings and pour in the miso. Cover well and simmer 45 minutes or until the zucchini is tender.

Rabbit casserole

Serves 2

450 g/1 lb rabbit portions
2–4 carrots, pared and cubed
4 prunes
4 or 6 large mushrooms, sliced
225 g/½ lb kohlrabi, rutabaga or turnip, pared and cubed

30 g/2 tbsp brown rice miso mixed to a thick paste in a little water
¼ tsp mixed herbs
salt and pepper
2–3 tsp millet flour

Preheat oven to 350 °F/180 °C.

Place all the ingredients in a suitably sized casserole with 120 ml/½ cup water and cook for 1¼–1½ hours.

Thicken the gravy by mixing the millet flour to a paste with a little water and stirring it in. Cook for an additional 15 minutes.

Kidney supper

Serves 2

4 large or 6 small kidneys
½ medium-sized green pepper, chopped
2 small cloves garlic, crushed
30 ml/2 tbsp sunflower oil
4 medium-sized carrots, peeled and sliced

4 tomatoes, quartered
30 g/2 tbsp brown rice miso mixed to a thick paste with a little water
salt and pepper
1½ tsp chickpea flour (optional)

Skin the kidneys, cut lengthwise and remove the cores.

Fry the green pepper and garlic in the oil and then add the carrots and halved kidneys. When these are browned, add the tomatoes, miso, 300 ml/1¼ cups water and salt and pepper to taste. Simmer gently for 15 minutes or until cooked. If necessary thicken the sauce by mixing the chickpea flour into a paste with a little cold water, then pouring the hot sauce into it. Stir well and return to the pan to cook for another 2 minutes.

Serve in a ring of rice.

Roast chicken with sweet potato stuffing (*top and center*, see page 74), Amazing technicolor risotto (*bottom*, see page 75)

POULTRY AND GAME

Roast chicken with sweet potato stuffing

Serves 4　　　　See photograph, page 72　

Stuffing:
170 g/¾ cup cooked sweet potato
30 g/2 tbsp lightly ground millet
sprig parsley, chopped
¼ tsp dried sage
salt and pepper
milk substitute

1 roasting chicken weighing about
　2 kg/4½ lb
salt and pepper
vegetable oil (soy, sunflower,
　safflower)

Mash the sweet potato and stir in the millet, herbs, salt and pepper with enough milk substitute to give a firm consistency. Press into an oiled baking dish. Cover with foil.

Preheat oven to 400 °F/200 °C.

Remove the giblets from the chicken and wipe inside and out. Season the inside of the bird lightly and spread the breast with a little vegetable oil. Place in a roasting pan and sear in the hot oven for 10 minutes. Then reduce the heat to 350 °F/180 °C and cover the chicken with foil.

Cook for an additional 45–50 minutes, basting the chicken occasionally. Thirty minutes before the chicken is done, place the baking dish with the stuffing in the oven.

Culpepper's chicken　　　

Serves 2

1½ tbsp finely chopped parsley
2 large sprigs chives, finely chopped
15 g/1 tbsp Kosher margarine

2 chicken portions
salt and pepper

Mash together the herbs and margarine. Lift the skin of the chicken portions away from the flesh taking care not to break the skin. Gently pack half the herb mixture under the skin of each chicken portion. Lightly season the other side of the chicken portion and broil that first, then turn to broil the stuffed side (about 10 minutes on each side, or until done).

Amazing technicolor risotto

Serves 2   See photograph, page 72

150 g/¾ cup brown rice
15 ml/1 tbsp sunflower oil
1 clove garlic, crushed
100 g/½ cup cooked chicken, chopped
60 g/¼ cup each of green, red and
  yellow peppers, sliced

30 g/⅛ cup sliced mushrooms
3 tomatoes, chopped
100 g/½ cup frozen peas
salt and pepper

Cook the rice (see page 25).

While the rice is cooking, heat the oil in a pan and fry the garlic, chicken, peppers and mushrooms. When the vegetables are soft, add the tomatoes, peas, and a little water and salt and pepper to taste. Cook over a gentle heat, stirring frequently. Add the rice when done and mix well.

Serve with salad.

Caribbean chicken

Serves 2

2 chicken portions
salt and pepper
1 clove garlic, crushed⁻
⅛ tsp dried rosemary and ground
  ginger

180 ml/¾ cup unsweetened pineapple
  juice
1½ tsp millet flour to thicken sauce
chopped parsley to garnish

Preheat oven to 350 °F/180 °C.

Place the chicken in a casserole dish, sprinkle with seasonings, garlic and herbs and pour in the pineapple juice.

Bake for approximately ¾ hour in the covered casserole.

Lift the chicken out and put under a hot broiler to brown the skin. Meanwhile, mix the millet flour to a paste with a little water, add to the sauce and simmer for 1 minute. Pour the sauce over the chicken and garnish with parsley.

Serve with fresh green vegetables or a salad.

Chickpea chicken supper

Serves 2

100 g/½ cup dry weight chickpeas,
  soaked overnight in water
30 g/2 tbsp brown rice miso dissolved
  in 300 ml/1¼ cups hot water
300 ml/1¼ cups apple juice
2 cloves garlic, crushed
¼ tsp dried rosemary

2 bay leaves
⅛ tsp cumin
225 g/½ lb pork steak, cubed
2 chicken drumsticks
salt and pepper
30 g/2 tbsp millet flour mixed to a
  paste in water

Drain the chickpeas and cook in plenty of boiling water for 1 hour (10 minutes in a pressure cooker at high pressure). They will not be completely cooked. Drain.

Mix all the ingredients together except for the millet flour and cook for 1¼–1½ hours, or 15 minutes in a pressure cooker. Thicken the gravy with the millet flour paste. Simmer uncovered for 5 minutes. Remove bay leaves and serve.

This dish is good served with spinach.

Spicy turkey

Serves 2

60 g/¼ cup green pepper, coarsely chopped
45 g/¾ cup mushrooms, chopped
45 ml/3 tbsp sunflower oil
2 turkey fillets
60 g/4 tbsp millet flour
⅛ tsp ground ginger

⅛ tsp ground nutmeg
15 g/1 tbsp brown rice miso dissolved in 150 ml/⅝ cup warm water
60 ml/¼ cup milk substitute
salt and pepper
toasted flaked almonds to garnish

Fry the green pepper and mushroom in the oil until soft. Move to one side of the pan and briskly fry the turkey until sealed.

Lift the turkey out and keep hot. Stir the millet, ginger and nutmeg into the oil, green pepper and mushroom mixture and cook for 1 minute. Gradually stir in the miso mixture and milk. Return the turkey and adjust the seasoning. Cover and simmer for 20–30 minutes or until the turkey is cooked through.

Serve garnished with the almonds.

Indian spiced chicken and tomatoes

Serves 2

30 ml/2 tbsp sunflower oil
4 cloves garlic, crushed (or less according to taste)
280 g/1¾ cups boned raw chicken, cubed
1 tsp ground coriander
1 tsp cumin
½ tsp turmeric

¼ tsp cayenne pepper
225 g/1 cup tomatoes, skinned and coarsely chopped
90 ml/6 tbsp chicken stock (see page 79)
1 tsp garam masala
salt

Heat oil in a skillet and lightly brown the garlic. Add the chicken, coriander, cumin, turmeric and cayenne pepper and fry, stirring, for 1 minute. Add the tomatoes and squash to a pulp. Add chicken stock and simmer for 15 minutes or until the chicken is cooked through. Stir in the garam masala and salt to taste.

Serve with rice or chickpea flour flatbread (see page 91) and raita (see page 86).

Variation Any other meat can be substituted for chicken in the recipe.

Oriental chicken

Serves 2

150 g/¾ cup brown rice
1 tsp tomato paste
2 cloves garlic, crushed
2 portions chicken, boned and cubed
1 green chili, seeded and finely chopped
60 g/⅔ cup okra, chopped

15–30 ml/1–2 tbsp sunflower oil
30 g/3 tbsp golden raisins
3 tomatoes, chopped
¼ tsp ground ginger
salt and pepper
cucumber rings to garnish

Cook the rice (see page 25). When done, stir in the tomato paste.

Fry the garlic, chicken, chili and okra in the oil. When the chicken and okra are almost cooked, add 150 ml/⅝ cup water, raisins, tomatoes, ginger, salt and pepper and simmer until cooked through.

Serve the chicken in a ring of rice and garnish with cucumber rings.

Mango chutney is a good accompaniment. (Choose one that is preservative and coloring-free).

Chicken liver with mushrooms

Serves 4

340 g/¾ lb chicken liver
15 ml/1 tbsp sunflower oil
60 g/⅓ cup chopped green pepper
15 g/1 tbsp gren chili pepper, seeded and chopped
2 cloves garlic, crushed
10 g/1 tbsp chickpea flour
6–8 tomatoes, quartered

15 ml/1 tbsp tomato paste dissolved in 120 ml/½ cup water
1 tsp dried mixed herbs
salt and pepper
130 g/2 cups button mushrooms, sliced
150 ml/⅝ cup apple juice

Remove any discolored patches and fibers from the livers and chop them roughly.

Heat the oil in a pan, add the green pepper, chili pepper and garlic and cook until soft. Dust the chicken livers in seasoned chickpea flour. Move the peppers to one side of the pan, and fry the livers quickly until lightly browned.

Add the tomatoes, diluted tomato paste solution, herbs, salt and pepper. Bring to a boil and simmer uncovered for 20 minutes.

Add the mushrooms and apple juice and cook for an additional 5–10 minutes.

This dish is good served on buckwheat pancakes (see page 45).

Turkey with apple and cherries

Serves 2   See photograph, page 81

2 turkey breasts
15 ml/1 tbsp sunflower oil
1 clove garlic, crushed
⅓ medium-sized green pepper, chopped
10 g/1 tbsp chickpea flour
30 g/2 tbsp brown rice miso dissolved
  in 300 ml/1¼ cups hot water

30 ml/2 tbsp apple juice
2 tsp red currant jelly
1 medium-sized cooking apple, pared
  and chopped
100 g/¾ cup cherries, washed and
  stoned
salt and pepper

Broil the turkey portions.

Heat the oil in a large skillet and fry the garlic and green pepper for 1 minute. Turn down the heat and stir in the chickpea flour and cook for another minute. Stir the miso mixture gradually into the flour and green pepper paste. Stir in the apple juice and red currant jelly. Add the apple and cherries. Season with salt and pepper.

Transfer the turkey and its juices from the broil pan to the skillet. Cover and simmer gently for an additional 5–10 minutes.

Scarecrow's favorite

Serves 2

2 small oven-ready game birds (frozen
  birds are usually available)
30 g/2 tbsp Kosher margarine
60 g/1 cup chopped mushrooms
2 small bay leaves

22 ml/1½ tbsp red currant jelly
6 peppercorns
salt and pepper
2 tbsp soy flour
watercress to garnish

Wash and dry the birds. Fry in margarine until browned. Add mushrooms, bay leaves, red currant jelly, peppercorns, salt and pepper and about 600 ml/2½ cups water. Cover and simmer for 1–1½ hours or until birds are cooked.

Remove the birds from the pan. Mix the soy flour to a paste with a little cold water and stir into the gravy. Simmer for an additional 5 minutes.

Garnish the birds with watercress, and serve with the thickened gravy and extra red currant jelly.

STOCKS, BATTERS, SAUCES AND SALAD DRESSINGS

Stocks   ★   W   M   E

Vegetable stock   An economical substitute for stock is the water in which any allowed vegetables have been cooked.

Use vegetable leftovers and discards such as the outer leaves of cabbage or spinach. Wash and store in the refrigerator in a plastic bag. When ready to make stock, chop the vegetables, just cover with lightly salted water and boil slowly for fifteen minutes to extract flavors, vitamins and minerals. Strain off the liquid and cool.

Meat or chicken stock   Use the raw bones of any suitable meat or poultry. Cover the bones with lightly salted cold water, bring to a boil and simmer for 3 hours, or cook in a pressure cooker for 30 minutes. Strain off the liquid and allow to cool, then skim fat.

Store any unused stock in the refrigerator, or freeze it.

Gravies   ★   W   M   E

Vegetable purées can be used in place of conventional gravy mixes, bouillon cubes or instant gravies. For convenience the purées can be made in bulk and frozen in smaller quantities for later use.

Examples
1. Red cabbage and mushrooms with sea salt and black pepper cooked with a knob of Kosher margarine and a little water until soft, then put through a blender, makes a rich replacement for gravy.
2. Skinned tomatoes, leeks, basil and sugar cooked together until soft, then put through a blender, makes a sweet sauce, ideal for lamb and ground beef dishes.
3. Carrots, celery and leeks with parsley cooked until soft, then put through a blender, makes a good accompaniment to chicken, turkey or egg dishes.

To color gravies, sauces and soups use gravy browning made from caramelized sugar (see overleaf).

Gravy browning

Makes about 150 ml/⅝ cup

120 g/½ cup sugar   *approximately 150 ml/⅝ cup water*

Dissolve the sugar in 2 tbsp water. Boil quickly until it is a dark brown liquid. Add a little water and heat gently until the caramel dissolves. Then add enough water to make a thin syrup. Bring to a boil, cool and bottle.

Only a small amount is needed to add color to gravies.

Tahini gravy

Makes about 300 ml/1¼ cups

15 ml/1 tbsp oil   *300 ml/1¼ cups water*
10 g/1 tbsp rice flour   *1 tsp brown rice miso, mixed to a thick*
1½ tsp tahini   *paste with a little water*

Heat the oil in a pan. Add rice flour and tahini. Mix until a thick paste is formed. Slowly add water and miso and stir until a thick brown gravy is formed. A little homemade gravy browning (see above) can be added to give a richer color.

Good with vegetarian dishes.

Coating batter

Makes about 150 ml/⅝ cup

(1)

120 g/¾ cup rice flour   *150 ml/⅝ cup milk substitute*
⅛ tsp sea salt   *1 tsp commercial wheat-free baking*
15 g/1 tbsp Kosher margarine melted   *powder (see page 89)*
in a saucepan or 15 ml/1 tbsp oil

Sift flour and salt together. Mix to a smooth consistency with the margarine or oil and milk and beat well.

Leave to stand for 30 minutes before using.

Just before using, stir in the baking powder.

(2)

120 g/¾ cup rice flour   *1 egg*
⅛ tsp salt   *150 ml/⅝ cup milk substitute*

Turkey with apple and cherries (*bottom*, see page 78), Tossed green salad
OVERLEAF: Strawberry ice (*top left*, see page 106), Rhubarb fool (*top right*, see page 106), Apricot mold (*bottom left*, see page 106), Gingered-up pears (*bottom right*, see page 109)

Sift flour and salt together. Make a well in the center of the flour and add the egg and milk. Mix to a smooth consistency and beat well.

Leave to stand for 30 minutes before using.

Suggestions for use   Coating for fried fish, fritters made with apple, banana or pineapple. (See photograph opposite)

Note: An excellent batter can also be made using chickpea flour; see recipe for pakoras (page 59) – spices can be omitted.

Basic white sauce

Makes about 60 ml/¼ cup

15 g/1 tbsp Kosher margarine   *60–90 ml/¼–⅓ cup milk substitute*
15 g/2 tbsp soy flour   *salt and pepper*

Melt the margarine over low heat, add the flour and stir well. Let the mixture cook slowly for 2 minutes. Then gradually add the warmed milk substitute stirring all the time to prevent lumps and let it simmer gently for 2 minutes (if the sauce is too thick, add a little extra milk substitute). Add salt and pepper, stir well and serve.

Basic tomato sauce

Makes about 340 g/1½ cups

450 g/1 lb tomatoes   *1 clove garlic, crushed*
15 ml/1 tbsp oil (olive, sunflower, saf-   *basil to taste*
flower, soy)   *salt and pepper*

Pour boiling water over the tomatoes, then drain after 1 minute. Plunge into cold water, drain and peel. Chop the tomatoes and place in a saucepan with oil, garlic, basil and seasoning. Simmer gently for 15 minutes.

Allow to cool and purée in an electric blender.

Reheat before serving.

This sauce is good with lamb, ground beef, pasta dishes, pizza, vegetables and legumes. It may be frozen.

Fruit fritters (bananas, pineapple, apple, *top*), Chickpea flour flatbread (*bottom right*, see page 91), Crusty rolls (*bottom left*, see page 91)

Tomato catsup

★ W M E

Serves 8

45 ml/3 tbsp tomato paste
45 ml/3 tbsp apple juice
10 g/1 tbsp chickpea flour
15 ml/1 tbsp sunflower oil
salt and pepper
⅛ chili powder

Mix all ingredients together and season.

Raita See photograph, page 54

W M E

Serves 4

480 ml/2 cups yogurt – goat's or ewe's
2 medium-sized onions, finely chopped or 1 cucumber, diced
2 tbsp chopped mint
⅛ tsp ground cumin
⅛ tsp chili powder
salt and freshly ground black pepper

Beat all the ingredients together to make a smooth, creamy texture. If desired, crushed garlic may also be added.

Serve with Indian dishes such as pakoras and chickpea flour flat bread.

Eggless mayonnaise

W M E

Makes about 240 ml/1 cup

½ tsp sea salt
1 tsp superfine sugar
1 tsp dry mustard – wheat-free pepper
10 g/1 tbsp rice flour
1 tsp arrowroot
60 ml/4 tbsp oil (sunflower, safflower, olive, soy)
60 ml/4 tbsp vinegar
210 ml/⅞ cup milk substitute

Mix salt, sugar, mustard, pepper and flours in a saucepan. Stir in oil. Add the vinegar gradually and finally the milk substitute. Bring to a boil stirring all the time and cook until the sauce has thickened. Adjust seasoning when cold.

Salad dressing

★ W M E

Combine equal quantities of apple juice and olive oil. Beat to an emulsion, add a few grains of white sugar and salt and pepper to taste.

Yogurt salad dressing   ✷ W M E

Makes about 150 ml/⅝ cup

150 ml/⅝ cup natural yogurt – goat's
or ewe's
1 tbsp chopped mint or chives

1 clove garlic, crushed
sea salt
pepper

Mix all the ingredients together just before serving.

Yogurt curd cheese salad dressing

Serves 1   ✷ W M E

2 tsp sheep's yogurt curd cheese
2 tsp sunflower oil

salt and pepper
mixed herbs to taste

Mix the curd cheese into the oil with the back of a spoon. Add the seasoning and herbs, then dilute with water to suit your taste.
   Use immediately.

Cheesy salad dressing   ✷ W M E

Serves 1

15 g/2 tbsp feta cheese
2 tsp sunflower oil
2 tsp apple juice

salt and pepper
chopped chives

Mix the cheese and oil to a paste with the back of a spoon. Stir in the apple juice, seasoning and herbs.
   Use immediately to dress a green salad.

Tahini salad dressing   ✷ W M E

Makes about 120 ml/½ cup

1½ tsp tahini
60 ml/¼ cup sunflower oil
1 clove garlic, crushed
½ tsp basil
½ tsp sugar

½ tsp crushed mustard seeds
brown rice miso to taste – about ½ tsp
*   mixed to a thick paste with a*
*   little water*

Place the first six ingredients in a cup and stir well. Add miso and stir again.

BREAD AND PASTRY

Homemade bread

Many people using this book will have to eat wheat-free bread. This is more difficult to make than ordinary bread at first, and a few notes of warning are needed. However, there are a lot of tasty wheat-free loaves that can be successfully made with practice. We include a few in this book which we think are well worth the effort.

Yeast   This can be bought either fresh or dry. Fresh yeast, wrapped in plastic wrap or foil, will keep for four to five days in a cold place, a month in a refrigerator or a year in a freezer. Dry yeast will keep up to six months if stored in a cool place. Half the amount of dry yeast is needed to fresh yeast, so, if 30 g/2 tbsp of fresh yeast is needed, use 15 g/2 packages active dry yeast. Temperature is very important when making yeast mixtures. Warm liquid accelerates the rising process, but if boiling liquids are used the yeast will be killed, and cold liquid slows growth.

Rising time   This depends on the temperature of the mixture. It may take forty-five to sixty minutes in a warm place such as an unheated oven, two hours at room temperature. It is therefore better to go by the look of the mixture than try to time it. The mixture should double in volume before baking.

Dough   Wheat-free breads will form a batter or cake-like consistency when mixed rather than an ordinary dough. This is because the flours used lack gluten, the protein that provides the elasticity and structure in ordinary bread.

Baking   Bread is baked in a very hot oven 450 °F/230 °C to kill the yeast. Loaf pans should only be half filled with the dough to allow space for rising. When baked, the crust will be a golden brown color. Allow the bread to cool slightly before turning out of the baking pan.

Storage   Wheat-free breads tend to dry out quickly. Therefore store in a plastic bag for short periods or in a freezer for longer storage. If the bread is sliced before freezing a few slices can be taken out and thawed when needed.

Baking powder

Baking powder contains starch such as rice flour, cornstarch and frequently wheat flour. Always check the list of ingredients on any purchased baking powder to make sure it is safe for you. If you are unable to find a suitable baking powder, you can make your own:

Homemade wheat-free baking powder

60 g/⅓ cup rice flour   *130 g/¾ cup cream of tartar*
60 g/⅓ cup soda

Sift the ingredients together at least 3 times. Store in an airtight container in a dry place.

Note: The recipes in this book are made with commercial wheat-free baking powder. If using homemade, slightly more is required, eg, if 2 tsp baking powder is stated in the recipe, use 3 tsp homemade powder.

Rusks

Wheat-free bread   *30 ml/2 tbsp honey*
300 ml/1¼ cups milk substitute

Cut wheat-free bread into slices about 1 cm/½ in thick. Cut these into sticks and dip into a mixture of milk substitute and honey.
    Bake in a moderate oven until dry.
    Cool and store in an airtight container. This is a good way of using up stale bread.

Plain white bread

Makes 1 × 900 g/2 lb loaf

30 g/2 tbsp fresh yeast or 15 g/2   *60 g/½ cup soybean flour*
  packages active dry yeast   *120 g/¾ cup rice flour*
1 tsp sugar   *1 tsp salt*
30 g/2 tbsp Kosher margarine   *240 ml/1 cup milk substitute*
170 g/1½ cups millet flour

See breadmaking notes opposite.
    Sprinkle the yeast on a mixture of 90 ml/6 tbsp warm water and sugar. Allow to stand until the liquid froths, about 10–20 minutes.
    Add the margarine cut into small pieces, then the sifted flours,

salt and milk substitute. Beat until the mixture is smooth and creamy. Place the bowl in a plastic bag and allow to rise in a warm place.

Preheat oven to 450 °F/230 °C. Pour mixture into a well-greased 900 g/2 lb loaf pan and bake for 30 minutes.

Brown bread

Makes 1 × 900 g/2 lb loaf

30 g/2 tbsp fresh yeast or 15 g/2 packages active dry yeast
1 tsp sugar
30 g/2 tbsp Kosher margarine
170 g/1¾ cups buckwheat flour

170 g/1¼ cups potato flour
1 tsp carob flour
1 tsp salt
180 ml/¾ cup milk substitute
1 egg

See breadmaking notes (page 88).

Sprinkle the yeast on to 90 ml/6 tbsp warm water and sugar. Allow to stand until the mixture froths, about 10–20 minutes.

Add the margarine cut into small pieces then the sifted flours, salt, milk substitute and egg. Beat until the mixture is smooth. Place the bowl in a plastic bag and allow to rise in a warm place.

Preheat oven to 450 °F/230 °C. Pour mixture into a well-greased 900 g/2 lb loaf pan and bake for 30 minutes.

Potato-rice flour bread

Makes 1 × 450 g/1 lb loaf

15 g/1 tbsp fresh yeast or 7 g/1 package active dry yeast
½ tsp sugar
85 g/⅔ cup potato flour

85 g/¾ cup rice flour
½ tsp salt
15 g/1 tbsp Kosher margarine

See breadmaking notes (page 88).

Mix yeast with sugar and 180 ml/¾ cup warm water. Leave to froth for 10–20 minutes. Sift the flours and salt together. Add margarine cut into small pieces and yeast mixture. Beat well. Place bowl in a plastic bag and leave to rise in a warm place.

Preheat oven to 450 °F/230 °C. Pour mixture into a greased 450 g/1 lb loaf pan and bake for 30 minutes.

Variation   For a wheat-free and milk-free loaf, reduce the water to 150 ml/⅝ cup and add 1 egg to the flour at the same time as the yeast mixture.

Crusty rolls See photograph, page 84

Makes 9 small rolls

*15 g/1 tbsp fresh yeast or 7 g/1
 package active dry yeast
½ tsp sugar
15 g/1 tbsp Kosher margarine
60 g/6 tbsp potato flour*

*60 g/½ cup rice flour
60 g/½ cup soy flour
½ tsp salt
1 egg
sesame seeds*

See breadmaking notes (page 88).

Sprinkle the yeast on to 150 ml/⅝ cup warm water and sugar mixture. Allow to stand and froth for about 10–20 minutes.

Add the margarine cut into small pieces, the sifted flours, salt and egg. Beat until the mixture is smooth and creamy. Place the bowl in a plastic bag and leave to rise in a warm place.

Preheat oven to 450 °F/230 °C. Spoon the dough into greased muffin pans and sprinkle with sesame seeds. Bake for 15 minutes.

Rice loaf

Makes 1 × 900 g/2 lb loaf

*150 ml/⅝ cup sunflower, safflower or
 soy oil
170 g/¾ cup superfine sugar
3 large beaten eggs*

*250 g/2¼ cups rice flour
2 tsp commercial wheat-free baking
 powder (see page 89)
15–30 ml/1–2 tbsp milk substitute*

Preheat oven to 350 °F/180 °C.

Grease a 900 g/2 lb loaf pan.

Beat oil and sugar together. Add the beaten egg a little at a time. Beat in sifted flour and baking powder. Add milk substitute to give a dropping consistency and beat well.

Pour into prepared pan and bake for 1–1½ hours.

Leave in pan until cool and then turn out.

Chickpea flour flatbread

Makes 4–6 See photograph, page 84

*2 tsp oil + oil for frying
120 g/1 cup chickpea flour
¼ tsp salt
and either
⅛ tsp chili powder (or to taste)*

*1 tsp cumin
or
any selection of chopped mixed fresh
 herbs, eg, parsley, chives
a little rice flour*

Rub 2 tsp oil into flour. Add salt and spices or herbs. Work into a dough with approximately 60 ml/¼ cup water. Divide into 4 or 6 balls. Roll out into flat circles on a board dusted with rice flour.

Fry in a little oil until brown on both sides.

Serve hot.

Fruit scones

Makes 12–15

225 g/2 cups sago or rice flour
2 tsp commercial wheat-free baking powder (see page 89)
60 g/4 tbsp Kosher margarine

60 g/¼ cup sugar
60 g/⅓ cup dried fruit
1 egg
60 ml/¼ cup milk substitute

Preheat oven to 450 °F/230 °C.

Sift flour and baking powder together and rub in marga. ne. Add the sugar and dried fruit and mix together to a soft dough with the lightly beaten egg and milk.

Drop the mixture with a tablespoon on to a greased baking sheet. Brush lightly with beaten egg or milk and bake for 15–20 minutes.

Apple-walnut tea bread

Makes 1 × 900 g/2 lb loaf

120 g/¾ cup potato flour
120 g/1 cup rice flour
1 tsp commercial wheat-free baking powder (see page 89)
⅛ tsp salt
1 level tsp allspice
120 g/½ cup Kosher margarine

120 g/⅔ cup superfine sugar
2 large eggs
15 ml/1 tbsp golden syrup or honey
120 g/¾ cup golden raisins
60 g/½ cup well chopped walnuts
1 cooking apple, pared, cored and chopped

Preheat oven to 325 °F/160 °C.

Grease a 900 g/2 lb loaf pan and line the base with waxed paper.

Sift flours, baking powder, salt and allspice.

Cream margarine and sugar together. Beat in 1 egg, syrup and 1 tbsp mixed flours. Beat in second egg and stir in the remainder of the flour, fruit, walnuts and apple. Place mixture in pan and level it. Bake for 1–1½ hours.

Turn out when cool and dust with confectioner's sugar.

Apple-walnut tea bread (*top*), Pear-carob cake (*center left*, see page 99), Plum bake (*center right*, see page 96)

Shortcrust pastry ⊠ W M E

To cover 1 × 22.5 cm/9 in pie dish

170 g/1½ cups chickpea flour
⅛ tsp salt
90 g/6 tbsp Kosher margarine
15–30 ml/1–2 tbsp ice water

Mix the flour and salt together. Cut the margarine into small pieces and rub it into the flour until the mixture resembles fine bread crumbs. Mix in water with a round-bladed knife until the mixture begins to stick together. Collect the mixture together with one hand, and knead lightly for a few seconds.

Roll out the dough in one direction only, on a floured surface, using chickpea flour.

Bake for 15–20 minutes in a preheated 425 °F/220 °C oven. Use as required.

Sweet shortcrust pastry ⊠ W M E

To cover 1 × 22.5 cm/9 in pie dish

170 g/1½ cups chickpea flour
60 g/6 tbsp superfine sugar
90 g/6 tbsp Kosher margarine
15–30 ml/1–2 tbsp ice water

Sift together the dry ingredients and rub in the margarine. Gradually stir in ice water to produce a suitable consistency for rolling out.

Bake for 15–20 minutes in a preheated 425 °F/220 °C oven. Use as required.

Buckwheat pastry ⊠ W M E

To cover 2 × 22.5 cm/9 in pie dishes

225 g/1 cup Kosher margarine
22–30 ml/1½–2 tbsp water
⅛ tsp salt
180 g/1½ cups buckwheat flour
180 g/1½ cups rice flour
1½ tsp cream of tartar
¾ tsp baking soda

Use margarine straight from the refrigerator. Cream the margarine, water, salt and one-third of the sifted flours in a mixing bowl. Mix in the remaining flour, cream of tartar and baking soda and knead until smooth, adding more water if necessary. Roll out thinly on a floured surface, using rice flour.

Bake for 20 minutes in a preheated 425 °F/220 °C oven.

Good with both sweet and savory pie fillings.

Fruit tart (*top*, see page 107), Millet and date buns (*center*, see page 100), Crunchy ginger slices (*bottom*, see page 102)

CAKES, CRACKERS
AND COOKIES

Plum bake See photograph, page 93

Serves 4

110 g/½ cup Kosher margarine
100 g/7 tbsp superfine sugar
1 medium-sized egg
30 g/3 tbsp potato flour
60 g/⅓ cup ground rice

30 g/¼ cup soy flour
½ tsp commercial wheat-free baking
    powder (see page 89)
8 plums

Preheat oven to 350 °F/180 °C.
    Cream the margarine and 6 tbsp sugar together. Beat in the egg.
Stir in the sifted flours and baking powder. Spread the mixture on
to a greased 18 cm/7 in square pan.
    Halve and pit the plums and press the halves into the surface of
the mixture. Sprinkle with the remaining sugar.
    Bake for 35–40 minutes or until firm when pressed in
center.
    Cut into squares when hot and serve warm with goat's or ewe's
yogurt, or cool and serve as a cake.

Variation Dried apricots (soaked and cooked) can be substituted for plums.

Spicy honey cake

85 g/4 tbsp clear honey
120 g/1 cup rice flour
60 g/6 tbsp potato flour
60 g/½ cup soy flour
1 level tsp ground ginger
1 level tsp ground cinnamon
¼ tsp ground cloves
85 g/6 tbsp superfine sugar
finely grated rind of 1 small orange
finely grated rind of 1 small lemon
110 g/½ cup Kosher margarine

1 large egg, beaten
1 level tsp baking soda, dissolved in 3
    tbsp water
60 g/⅓ cup mixed candied peel,
    finely chopped

Icing:
120 g/1 cup confectioner's sugar
22 ml/1½ tbsp lemon juice
30 ml/2 tbsp warm water

Preheat oven to 325 °F/160 °C.
    Measure the honey into a cup. Place the cup in a saucepan con-
taining simmering water and warm the honey a little.

Sift the flours and spices into a large mixing bowl, then add sugar and the orange and lemon rinds. Add the margarine in small pieces and rub it into the flours until it resembles fine bread crumbs. Mix in the beaten egg using a large fork, and then add the honey. Add the baking soda in water to cake mixture. Beat well until the mixture is smooth and soft.

Stir in the mixed peel and spoon the mixture into an 18 cm/7 in square greased pan. Bake for 45 minutes. Cool before turning out on to a wire rack.

Prepare the icing and spread it over the cooled cake.

Sponge cake

4 eggs
110 g/½ cup superfine sugar
110 g/1 cup sago flour
1 tsp commercial wheat-free baking powder (see page 89)

Fillings:
stewed apple, nut cream (see page 110), jam or any other filling allowed

Preheat oven to 350 °F/180 °C.

Grease two 20 cm/8 in layer cake pans.

Place the eggs and sugar in a bowl over a pan of hot water. Beat until thick and creamy. Fold in sifted flour and baking powder. Divide the mixture between the pans and bake for 25–30 minutes until golden brown.

When cool, sandwich together with chosen filling.

Variation   Rice flour can be substituted for sago flour.

Gingerbread

225 g/2 cups rice flour
2½ tsp ground ginger
1¼ tsp allspice
¾ tsp baking soda
2 tsp commercial wheat-free baking powder (see page 89)
120 ml/½ cup golden or corn syrup

35 ml/2 tbsp + 1 tsp sunflower, safflower or soya oil
35 g/2½ tbsp superfine sugar
35 ml/2 tbsp + 1 tsp milk substitute
20 ml/1 rounded tbsp blackstrap molasses
1 large egg, beaten

Preheat oven to 350 °F/180 °C.

Sift the flour, ginger, allspice, baking soda and baking powder into a bowl. Make a well in the center. Melt the syrup, oil and sugar in a pan over a low heat. Pour on to the flour mixture. Add milk, molasses and egg. Beat until smooth. Pour into a greased 20 cm/8 in pan. Bake for 1 hour.

Turn out on to a wire rack and cool.

Ground rice cake

110 g/½ cup Kosher margarine
110 g/½ cup superfine sugar
2 eggs
110 g/⅔ cup ground rice
60 g/⅜ cup potato flour

grated rind of 1 lemon
juice of ½ lemon
½ tsp baking soda stirred into 1 tsp
  milk substitute

Preheat oven to 350 °F/180 °C.
 Cream the margarine and sugar together. Add 1 egg. Combine the flours and stir in 1 tsp of flour mixture. Add the second egg and lemon rind and mix. Add remainder of flour and lemon juice. Mix well with the baking soda in milk substitute.
 Place in a greased 20 cm/8 in cake pan and bake for 1¼ hours.

Snow cake

110 g/½ cup Kosher margarine
110 g/½ cup superfine sugar
2 eggs

225 g/1½ cups potato flour
1 tsp commercial wheat-free baking
  powder (see page 89)

Preheat oven to 325 °F/160 °C.
 Cream margarine and sugar together. Add eggs and potato flour. Stir in the baking powder. Beat for 10 minutes.
 Pour into a shallow 18 × 28 cm/7 × 11 in baking pan, greased and lightly floured. The mixture should cover the pan to a depth of about 1 cm/½ in. Bake for 30 minutes.
 Turn out when cool. Spread with icing (lemon-flavored is very good), and cut into bars.

Buckwheat cake

150 ml/⅝ cup thin honey
150 ml/⅝ cup sunflower oil
2 eggs

170 g/1½ cups buckwheat flour
4½ tsp commercial wheat-free baking
  powder (see page 89)

Preheat oven to 325 °F/160 °C.
 Grease and flour an 18 cm/7 in cake pan.
 Beat together honey, oil and eggs. Sift together flour and baking powder at least twice. Beat the dry ingredients into the first mixture. Pour the mixture into prepared cake pan.
 Bake for 50–60 minutes.

Carob cake

150 ml/⅝ cup thin honey
150 ml/⅝ cup sunflower oil
2 eggs

170 g/1½ cups carob flour
4½ tsp commercial wheat-free baking
  powder (see page 89)

Preheat oven to 325 °F/160 °C.

Beat together the honey, oil and eggs. Sift together flour and baking powder at least twice. Beat the dry ingredients into the first mixture.

Pour into 2 prepared 18 cm/7 in cake pans. Bake for 1 hour.

Allow to cool, and sandwich together either with confectioner's sugar creamed with Kosher margarine, and softened with a little milk substitute if necessary, or with homemade or preservative-free commercial jam.

Buckwheat fruit cake

110 g/1 cup rice flour
110 g/1 cup buckwheat flour
110 g/½ cup Kosher margarine
110 g/½ cup brown sugar
2 tsp commercial wheat-free baking
powder (see page 89)
120 g/⅔ cup golden raisins and currants mixed
60 g/⅓ cup chopped dates
milk substitute to mix

Preheat oven to 350 °F/180 °C.

Sift flours into a bowl. Rub in margarine until it resembles fine bread crumbs. Add sugar, baking powder and dried fruit and enough milk substitute to give a stiff consistency.

Place into a greased 15 cm/6 in cake pan. Bake for 1 hour.

Variation Can be made entirely with rice flour.

Pear-carob cake

See photograph, page 93

110 g/½ cup Kosher margarine
150 g/1¼ cups rice flour
30 g/4 tbsp carob flour
85 g/¾ cup soy flour
120 g/½ cup brown sugar
2 pears, stewed, cooled and puréed
15–30 ml/1–2 tbsp milk substitute
1 level tsp baking soda in 2 tsp water

Filling:
60 g/4 tbsp Kosher margarine
85 g/¾ cup confectioner's sugar

Preheat oven to 350 °F/180 °C.

Rub margarine into flours, then add sugar. Mix thoroughly. Make a well in center and slowly stir in pears and milk substitute until all the flour has been used. The mixture should be slightly sloppy. Add baking soda. Beat the mixture well until it becomes smooth and fluffy. This is important: if the beating does not reach this stage, the cake will be flat and unpalatable.

Turn immediately into two 18 cm/7 in greased cake pans. Bake for 25–30 minutes.

For the filling, cream the margarine, add sugar gradually and beat together. When the cake is cool, sandwich the two halves together with the filling.

Apple cake   W M

450 g/1 lb cooking apples
170 g/¾ cup Kosher margarine
225 g/1 cup superfine sugar
2 large eggs
120 g/¾ cup potato flour
60 g/½ cup rice flour

60 g/½ cup soy flour
2 tsp commercial wheat-free baking
    powder (see page 89)
⅛ tsp salt
ground cinnamon to taste

Preheat oven to 350 °F/180 °C.
   Pare, core and cut apples into slices. Cook very gently in 30 g/2 tbsp margarine until apple is approximately half-cooked. Remove from heat.
   Cream rest of margarine and sugar together. Beat the eggs into the mixture. Fold in the sifted flours, baking powder and salt. Place half the cake mixture into a greased cake pan 23 cm/9 in in diameter. Arrange the apple slices over this and sprinkle with cinnamon. Cover with the remaining cake mixture. Bake for 1½ hours.
   Cool slightly before removing from the pan. Dust with confectioner's sugar when completely cool.

Millet and date buns   W M

Makes 12–16 buns   See photograph, page 94

225 g/2¼ cups millet flour
4 tsp commercial wheat-free baking
    powder (see page 89)
60 g/4 tbsp Kosher margarine

60 ml/¼ cup milk substitute
2 eggs
60 g/¼ cup sugar
120 g/⅔ cup chopped dates

Preheat oven to 425 °F/220 °C.
   Sift flour and baking powder together; rub in margarine. Mix milk substitute, eggs, sugar and dates together and add to the flour. Beat to a stiff consistency. Spoon into greased muffin pans or paper cases. Bake for 15–20 minutes.

Variations   Omit dates and add any one of the following.
Carob buns: use 200 g/1¾ cups millet flour and 30 g/¼ cup carob flour.
Coconut buns: add 60 g/⅝ cup flaked coconut to the mixture.
Ginger buns: add 2 tsp ground ginger to the flour.
Seed buns: add 1½ tsp caraway seeds to the mixture.

Rice Krispie cakes   ★ W M E

Makes 20–24 cakes

30 ml/2 tbsp honey or golden syrup
30 g/2 tbsp brown sugar

at least 30 g/1 cup Rice Krispies

Heat honey and sugar until sugar dissolves. Stir in enough Rice Krispies to absorb the honey. Spoon into paper cases and leave to cool and harden.

Variations Chopped dates or 2 tsp carob flour may be added.

Buckwheat crackers

Makes 8–10 crackers

100 g/1 cup buckwheat flour
⅛ tsp salt
1½ tsp commercial wheat-free baking powder (see page 89)

30 g/2 tbsp Kosher margarine
60 ml/¼ cup milk substitute

Preheat oven to 375 °F/190 °C.
  Sift together flour, salt and baking powder at least twice. Rub in the margarine. Make a well in the center and gradually pour in the milk, stirring to form a soft dough.
  Turn on to a floured board and roll out to 1 cm/½ in thick. Cut into circles, arrange on a greased baking sheet and bake for 10–15 minutes.
  These are good to use in packed lunches.

Buckwheat and rice crackers

Makes 15–20 crackers

150 g/⅝ cup Kosher margarine
110 g/1 cup rice flour
110 g/1 cup buckwheat flour

⅛ tsp salt
1 tsp cream of tartar
½ tsp baking soda

Preheat oven to 350 °F/180 °C.
  In a mixing bowl cream the margarine with 1–1½ tsp water, salt and one-third of the flours (for best results use margarine straight from the refrigerator). Mix in the remaining flour, cream of tartar and baking soda until smooth. Add more water if necessary to make a soft dough.
  Roll out the dough thinly on a floured surface. Cut into squares and place on a greased baking sheet. Bake for about ½ hour until brown.
  These are very good with goat's cheese.

Shortbread

Makes 8–10 pieces

85 g/¾ cup soy flour
85 g/¾ cup rice flour
60 g/¼ cup superfine or granulated sugar

110 g/½ cup Kosher margarine
30 ml/2 tbsp milk substitute

Preheat oven to 325 °F/160 °C.

Grease and flour a 18 cm/7 in square or circular shallow pan.

Sift together the soy and rice flours, then sift with the sugar. Rub in the margarine and stir in the milk substitute. Mix lightly to form a dough and press into the pan to a thickness of about 1 cm/½ in. Prick surface with a fork.

Bake for 45 minutes.

Chestnut shortbread

Makes 10–15 pieces

60 g/½ cup chestnut flour
85 g/¾ cup ground rice
grated rind of 1 lemon

cinnamon or allspice to taste
1½ tsp fructose
15 ml/1 tbsp safflower oil

Preheat oven to 350 °F/180 °C.

Mix all the ingredients together and rub in the oil with fingertips. Gather lightly to form a dough and press into a greased 20 cm/8 in square or circular shallow pan to a thickness of about 1 cm/½ in. Prick the surface and bake for 20 minutes.

Iced gingersnaps

Makes 12–16

30 g/2 tbsp Kosher margarine
30 g/3 tbsp soft brown sugar
60 g/¼ cup golden syrup
60 g/½ cup soy flour
30 g/¼ cup rice flour

1 tsp commercial wheat-free baking
* powder (see page 89)*
½ tsp cream of tartar
½ tsp ground ginger
glacé icing

Preheat oven to 350 °F/180 °C.

Melt the margarine in a pan on low heat and stir in the golden syrup and sugar. Sift together the dry ingredients and then re-sift them into the pan. Stir to a firm paste. Take small spoonfuls and roll in the hands until smooth (walnut size), then flatten on a greased baking sheet. Bake for 15–17 minutes.

Leave to cool, then decorate with glacé icing.

Crunchy ginger slices

See photograph, page 94

110 g/½ cup Kosher margarine
110 g/½ cup sugar
60 g/½ cup soy flour
150 g/1 cup potato flour
1 tsp ground ginger
1 tsp commercial wheat-free baking
* powder (see page 89)*

Icing:
60 g/4 tbsp Kosher margarine
170 g/1½ cups confectioner's sugar
2 tsp ground ginger
15 ml/1 tbsp honey

Preheat oven to 375 °F/190 °C.

Cream margarine and sugar together. Add sifted flours, ginger and baking powder. Knead well.

Roll flat and press into a greased shallow pan 23 cm × 28 cm/9 in × 11 in.

Bake for 25 minutes and allow to cool.

To make the icing, melt all the ingredients in a saucepan. Pour it while still hot over the cake (makes a thick covering of icing). Cut into slices before the icing is completely cool.

Currant cookies

Makes about 16

30 g/2 tbsp Kosher margarine
30 g/2 tbsp light brown sugar
30 ml/2 tbsp golden syrup
110 g/1 cup rice flour

1 tsp commercial wheat-free baking
  powder (see page 89)
1 tsp cream of tartar
30 g/2 tbsp currants

Preheat oven to 350 °F/180 °C.

Melt margarine in a pan over a low heat and stir in sugar and golden syrup until dissolved. Combine dry ingredients and sift into pan. Mix to a firm paste, with the currants evenly distributed. Take small spoonfuls and roll until smooth – about the size of a whole walnut. Flatten and place well apart on a greased baking sheet.

Bake for 15–20 minutes and cool on baking sheet.

Best eaten within 48 hours.

Millet flake bars

110 g/½ cup Kosher margarine
60 g/¼ cup brown sugar

15 ml/1 tbsp thin honey
170 g/1¾ cups millet flakes

Preheat oven to 350 °F/180 °C.

Cream the margarine and sugar. Add the honey and millet flakes. Mix well.

Press into a greased baking pan 20 cm/8 in square. Bake for 15 minutes.

Mark into squares and allow to cool before lifting off the pan.

Rice Krispie cookies

Makes 12–16 small cookies

45 g/1½ cups Rice Krispies
2 egg whites
1½ tsp clear honey

60 g/¼ cup superfine sugar
parchment paper

Preheat oven to 375 °F/190 °C.

Place parchment paper on a baking sheet.

Crush the Rice Krispies with a rolling pin. Whisk egg whites until they are very stiff. Add honey and fold in sugar and Rice Krispies. Spoon on to parchment paper. Bake for 20–25 minutes.

Carob cookies

Makes 15–20 cookies

110 g/½ cup Kosher margarine
75 g/⅓ cup superfine sugar
200 g/1¾ cups rice flour

30 g/¼ cup carob flour
30 ml/2 tbsp oil
1 egg

Preheat oven to 350 °F/180 °C.

Cream margarine and 60 g/4 tbsp sugar together. Work in the sifted flours, oil and egg and knead well.

Roll out to ½ cm/¼ in thick, and cut into shapes. Prick each cookie with a fork and put on a baking sheet, oiled and dusted with rice flour. Bake for about 15 minutes until firm and crisp. Dust with remaining sugar while still warm.

Remove from baking sheet when cool.

FRUIT AND DESSERTS

Summer fruit dessert   ✷ W M E

Serves 4

1–2 nectarines
1–2 peaches
225 g/1 pint red or black currants,
  topped and tailed

225 g/1 pint raspberries or strawberries
sugar to taste

Stew the currants in 2 tbsp water and sweeten to taste. Allow to cool.

Wash the nectarines and peaches and slice into quarters.

Wash the berries.

Mix together and chill before serving.

Shortbread is a good accompaniment to this dessert (see page 101).

Anytime-of-year fruit salad ✴ Ⓦ Ⓜ Ⓔ

Serves 4–6

½ pineapple
1–2 bananas
1 eating apple from several different varieties, eg, McIntosh, Granny Smith, Golden Delicious

120 g/1 cup fresh or frozen raspberries or strawberries
335 g/2 cups gooseberries, fresh or canned
sugar (optional)

Cut the pineapple into coarse chunks. Be careful to cut out the eyes and to save all the juice for other dishes, or to drink. Peel and chop bananas. Core and slice apples. Mix all the fruits together and add sugar to taste if desired. Chill before serving.

Dried fruit compote ✴ Ⓦ Ⓜ Ⓔ

Serves 6

30 g/2 tbsp sugar
5–8 cm/2–3 in cinnamon stick
450 g/1 lb mixed dried fruit, eg, apple

rings, peaches, apricots, prunes, pears and golden raisins

Dissolve the sugar in 600 ml/2½ cups water over a gentle heat. Add the cinnamon. Place the dried fruit in a bowl and pour on the syrup. Cover and leave to soak overnight.

If the soaked fruit is not tender, place in a pan and simmer for a few minutes.

Serve cold with yogurt.

Fruit gelatin ✴ Ⓦ Ⓜ Ⓔ

Serves 4

20 g/3 envelopes unflavored gelatin
600 ml/2½ cups unsweetened fruit juice, eg, apple or pineapple

Sprinkle the gelatin on 90 ml/⅓ cup heated fruit juice, and stir well till dissolved. Add the rest of the juice. Put into a moistened mold and chill until set.

Variation This can be made with sweetened milk substitute to give a milk gelatin. Sprinkle the gelatin on to 4 tbsp water then heat gently to dissolve. Add the gelatin to 600 ml/2½ cups milk substitute while still hot but not boiling. The milk substitute may be flavored with vanilla if liked.

Strawberry ice   ⊠ Ⓦ Ⓜ Ⓔ

Serves 4–6   See photograph, page 82

280 g/1¼ cups strawberries, fresh or   *30 g/2 tbsp sugar*
  frozen   *15 g/2 envelopes unflavored gelatin*

Purée the strawberries and sugar together in an electric blender.
Dissolve the gelatin in 250 ml/1 cup warm water. Mix with the
fruit. Place in a freezer or freezer compartment of the refrigerator. When partially frozen, beat well, if possible with an
electric beater, then freeze until firm.

Rhubarb fool   ⊠ Ⓦ Ⓜ Ⓔ

Serves 2   See photograph, page 83

30 g/2 tbsp Kosher margarine   *30 g/2 tbsp brown sugar*
225 g/½ lb rhubarb   *200 ml/⅞ cup goat's or ewe's yogurt*

Melt the margarine in a pan. Add the rhubarb and sugar and cook
until tender. Purée rhubarb and yogurt together in an electric
blender.
  Chill before serving.

Apricot mold   ⊠ Ⓦ Ⓜ Ⓔ

Serves 4   See photograph, page 82

130 g/¾ cup dried apricots   *15 g/2 envelopes unflavored gelatin*
30 g/2 tbsp granulated sugar

Pour boiling water over apricots and leave to soak for several
hours. Drain and wash. Stew for 10 minutes until soft in 60 ml/¼
cup water. Sieve to make a purée, then stir in the sugar.
  Dissolve the gelatin in 90 ml/6 tbsp very hot water, stirring
briskly. Make up to 300 ml/1¼ cups with cold water, then stir into
the apricot mixture.
  Arrange the remaining apricots on the bottom of a moistened
mold, then carefully pour the mixture in. Chill in the refrigerator
for 3 hours.

Grantchester dessert   Ⓦ Ⓜ Ⓔ

Serves 1

15 ml/1 tbsp honey   *sprinkling of chopped almonds*
110 g/½ cup sheep's yogurt   *or fresh fruit*

Spoon the honey into the bottom of a custard cup and add the
yogurt. Garnish with nuts or fruit.

Peach condé

☒ W M E

Serves 6   See photograph, page 111

60 g/¼ cup short grain rice
600 ml/2½ cups milk substitute
60 g/¼ cup superfine sugar

1 can peaches (preservative-free) or 3
  fresh peaches
30 g/3 tbsp arrowroot

Wash the rice and simmer with the milk substitute until thick and creamy. Leave to cool. Add sugar.

Divide rice between six serving dishes. If using canned peaches, drain and place one peach half in each dish. Thicken the juice with arrowroot. If using fresh peaches, skin and halve and place one half in each dish. Make an arrowroot sauce with 300 ml/1¼ cups liquid, eg, apple juice. Pour the arrowroot sauce over the fruit and leave to set.

Rice flake mold

☒ W M E

Serves 4

85 g/2½ cups rice flakes
600 ml/2½ cups milk substitute

45 g/3 tbsp superfine sugar

Sprinkle rice flakes into nearly boiling milk substitute and cover pan with lid. Simmer until tender (10–15 minutes) and the milk almost absorbed. Sweeten with the sugar. Pour quickly into a cold, wet mold. Turn out when set, after about 2 hours.

Serve with stewed fruit.

Fruit tart

W M

Serves 4–5   See photograph, page 94

1 egg
75 ml/¼ cup clear honey
75 ml/⅓ cup sunflower oil
85 g/¾ cup buckwheat flour
2½ tsp commercial wheat-free baking
  powder (see page 89)

350 g/¾ lb rhubarb or other allowed
  fruit
30–45 g/2–3 tbsp sugar
15 g/2 envelopes unflavored gelatin
apple slices to garnish

Preheat oven to 325 °F/160 °C.

Blend together the egg, honey and sunflower oil. Sift in the buckwheat flour and baking powder. Mix well, then pour into a greased 18 cm/7 in pie plate. Bake for 30–35 minutes.

Meanwhile, stew the rhubarb, or whatever fruit you are using, with the sugar in a minimum of water.

Mix the gelatin in 150 ml/⅝ cup of very hot water. When it dissolves, make up to 300 ml/1¼ cups with cold water. Stir in the rhubarb and juice and place in a bowl to set.

When almost set, pile on to the pastry and decorate with apple slices just before serving.

Crispy caramel fruit

Serves 4

4 dessert apples
2 bananas

halved seeded black grapes
enough brown sugar to cover fruit

Pare and core the apples and stew in a little water until soft. Mash if necessary, and spoon into ovenproof ramekins or custard cups. Arrange sliced banana to cover as much as possible of the apple. Decorate with grape halves.

Sprinkle with sugar and place under a hot broiler until the sugar has melted, or bake in a hot oven for 10 minutes.

Stuffed baked apples

Serves 4

4 cooking apples
15 ml/1 tbsp honey

Stuffing:
dates, honey and ground cloves or cinnamon
or
raisins and brown sugar

Preheat oven to 400 °F/200 °C.

Core the apples and slit the skin in a ring round the middle. Stuff with chosen filling and place in a baking dish.

Add 5 mm/¼ in of water and 1 tbsp of honey to the baking dish. Bake until the fruit is tender.

Serve hot or cold.

Baked bananas

Serves 4

See photograph, page 111

4 bananas
45 g/3 tbsp Kosher margarine

60–85 g/¼–⅓ cup brown sugar

Preheat oven to 350 °F/180 °C.

Peel bananas and lay them in a flameproof dish. Sprinkle with 2 tbsp water. Cover each banana with several dots of margarine and sugar. Bake for 30 minutes.

Serve with goat's or ewe's milk·yogurt or nut cream (see page 110).

Gingered-up pears

Serves 2   See photograph, page 83

2 pears   *15 g/1 tbsp brown sugar*
15 g/½ cup fresh ginger root, peeled   *blanched almonds*
and finely chopped

Halve the pears lengthwise and carefully remove the core.
Arrange in the bottom of a medium-sized pan, cut surface on top,
pour on 60 ml/¼ cup water and add a quarter of the ginger. Gently
simmer with the lid on until the pears are just softening. Lift them
out carefully, place in serving dishes and keep warm.

To the juice in the pan add the rest of the ginger, 150 ml/⅝ cup
water and the sugar. Simmer for 5 minutes, then sieve.

Decorate the pears with the almonds, and serve the hot ginger
sauce separately.

Fruit crumble ★   E

Serves 4

60 g/⅓ cup ground rice   *60 g/½ cup soy flour*
60 g/½ cup rice flour   *with*
or   *60 g/4 tbsp Kosher margarine*
120 g/1 cup sago flour   *60 g/¼ cup brown sugar*
or   *450 g/1 lb any fruit, eg, apples,*
60 g/½ cup rice flour   *pears, plums*

Rub margarine into flour until it resembles fine bread crumbs.
Mix in the sugar.

Wash and slice the fruit, place in an ovenproof dish and add a
little sugar if necessary.

Place the crumbs on top of the fruit and bake in the oven at
375 °F/190 °C until brown on top.

Millet crisp ★ W M E

Serves 4

60 g/4 tbsp Kosher margarine   *or*
60 g/⅓ cup soft brown sugar   *plums and sugar*
120 g/1⅛ cups millet flakes   *or*
450 g/1 lb apples and golden raisins *rhubarb and dates*
with cinnamon   *or*
                                      bananas and figs

Cream the margarine and sugar together. Mix in the millet flakes.
Place on top of chosen fruit and bake in oven at 375 °F/190 °C until
brown on top.

Nut cream

Serves 2

60 g/½ cup mixed nuts   *water*

Grind nuts finely using the fine attachment on a meat grinder, or a coffee grinder. Mix with enough cold water to form a cream.
    Use as cream on fruit, salads or vegetables.

Note: By using different types of nuts the flavor of the cream can be varied.

Molasses toffee

Makes 250 g/9 oz

150 g/⅔ cup light brown sugar   *1½ tsp blackstrap molasses*
30 g/2 tbsp Kosher margarine   *1½ tsp golden syrup or corn syrup*
⅛ tsp cream of tartar

Dissolve the sugar in 50 ml/¼ cup water, using a heavy, large pan over a low heat. Add the other ingredients and bring to a boil. Do not stir the mixture. Boil to 250 °F/132 °C (when a small bit dropped into cold water separates into threads that are hard but not brittle). Pour into a greased pan. Cut into squares as it cools.

Peppermint creams

Makes 60

450 g/1 lb granulated sugar   *peppermint extract to taste*
⅛ tsp cream of tartar

Place 150 ml/⅝ cup water and the sugar in heavy-based aluminum pan and heat gently until the sugar has dissolved. Bring to a boil, add the cream of tartar and continue boiling the mixture to 235 °F/116 °C. To check the temperature, either use a thermometer, or wait until a bit of mixture dropped into very cold water forms a soft ball, which flattens on being removed from the water.
    Pour the mixture into a cool, large flat ovenproof dish or on to a marble slab. Work it back and forwards in a figure eight with a wooden spoon or spatula, adding peppermint extract as desired. The mixture will gradually become opaque and firm. Making sure your hands are very clean, not to discolor the mixture, knead until a suitable consistency to roll into individual candies. Form into a sausage shape about 2.5 cm/1 in in diameter and slice into disks about ½ cm/¼ in thick.

Baked bananas with nut cream (*top*, see page 108 and above), Peppermint creams (*centre*), Peach condé (*bottom*, see page 107).

ACKNOWLEDGMENTS

The authors would like to thank their families for putting up with them and for tasting the recipes, and Alison Wilson for keeping them sane and organized during the writing of this book.

1984   Elizabeth Workman, Virginia Alun Jones and
                                                    John Hunter

The publishers are grateful to the following for their help in the preparation of this book: the photographs were taken by Peter Myers, assisted by Neil Mersh; art direction was by Rose and Lamb Design Partnership, styling by Penny Markham and food preparation by Lisa Collard.

Allergy-free foods: (*clockwise*) Bananas, mango, guava, passion fruit, lychees, kiwi fruit, fennel, water chestnuts, sweet potato, celeriac, millet, okra, flaked and brown rice, selection of goat's cheese, feta, soya cheese

INDEX

Page numbers in *italic* refer to the illustrations